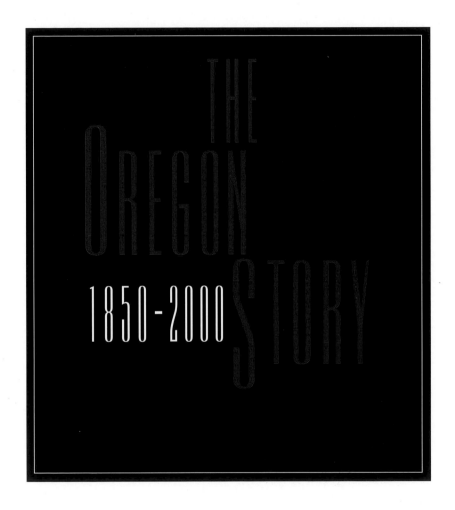

THE OREGON STORY

1850-2000

By the staff of

The Oregonian

Graphic Arts Center Publishing®

COPYRIGHT

Published by Graphic Arts Center Publishing®
An imprint of Graphic Arts Center Publishing Company
P.O. Box 10306, Portland, Oregon 97296-0306
503/226-2402
www.gacpc.com

Library of Congress Cataloging-in-Publication Data
available upon request.
International Standard Book Number: 1-55868-543-X

Graphic Arts Center Publishing Company
President: Charles M. Hopkins
Editorial Staff: Douglas A. Pfeiffer, Timothy W. Frew,
    Ellen Harkins Wheat, Tricia Brown, Jean Andrews,
    Alicia I. Paulson, and Jean Bond-Slaughter
Production Staff: Richard L. Owsiany, Heather Doornink,
    and Joanna Goebel
Designer: Deidra McQuiston Straka

The Oregonian
Publisher: Fred A. Stickel
President: Patrick F. Stickel
Editor: Sandra M. Rowe

The Oregon Story team
Editor: Michael Arrieta-Walden
Photo editor: Randy Rasmussen
Copy editors: Brian Harrah, Kathy Hinson, Jerry Sass,
    Holly Franko, and Kay Mitchell
Designer of original newspaper displays: Michelle Wise
Photo research: Randy Rasmussen, Contessa Williams,
    and John Meyers
Chronologies: John Terry
Research: Gail Hulden, Lovelle Svart, Margie Gultry,
    Kathleen Blythe, Marie Lewis, Carol McMenamin,
    and Nanette Lesage Robinson
Graphics: Dan Aguayo

Printed in Hong Kong

Above: *Broadway Theater, Portland, early 1940s.*
Title page: *Senator Mark Hatfield in Capitol in Washington, D.C., 1996.*
Contents page: *Umatilla Indian scouts, 1878.*

Acknowledgments

The Oregonian would like to acknowledge several historians, researchers and experts who made extraordinary efforts to help in the publication of this project.

Historians who provided guidance included Chet Orloff, executive director, Oregon Historical Society; Carl Abbott, Portland State University; Darrell Millner, Portland State University; Stephen Dow Beckham, Lewis and Clark College; Marianne Keddington-Lang, Oregon Historical Quarterly; David Horowitz, Portland State University; E. Kimbark MacColl; Linda Elegant, Portland Community College History Center; Ruth Barnes Moynihan; Jean M. Ward, Lewis & Clark; Robert Johnston, Yale University; William G. Robbins, Oregon State University; John Mack Faragher, Yale University; Terence O'Donnell; and Thomas Vaughan.

Others providing extra help were John Mitchell, western regional economist for U.S. Bancorp; Tom Potiowsky, chief state economist; Paul Warner, director of the state Legislative Revenue Office; Ernie Englander, George Washington University; Ed Klimasauskas, Cascades Volcano Observatory in Vancouver, Washington; Marjorie Waheneka, National Park Service; and Roy Keene, a Eugene forestry consultant.

Providing extensive research assistance were David Hopkins, Oregon Health Division; Cathy Riddell, Oregon Health Division; Brian White, Department of Environmental Quality; Richard H. Engeman, Oregon Historical Society; Mary Grant, Archdiocese of Portland in Oregon; Art Ayre, Oregon Employment Department; Jeff D. Bock, Law Enforcement Data System; Diana Banning, City of Portland archivist; and Kevin Beckstrom, Driver and Motor Vehicle Services.

Providing assistance with historical photos were photo librarians of the Oregon Historical Society; photographers Hugh Ackroyd and Jim Vincent; Buck Munger of Two Louies; and The Oregon Sports Hall of Fame Museum.

Photo Credits

CONTENTS

The steamboat *Bailey Gatzert* passes the Cascade Rapids on the Columbia River, circa 1890.

The Promise of Eden

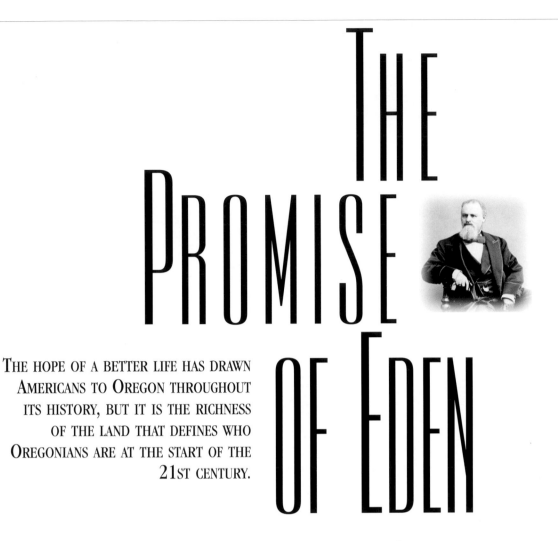

The hope of a better life has drawn Americans to Oregon throughout its history, but it is the richness of the land that defines who Oregonians are at the start of the 21st century.

By Brian Meehan

Before Oregon was a territory or even a destination on a long trail, it was an idea. And the idea—an Eden where people prospected not for gold but for a better life—became the lifeblood that nurtured the Beaver State to the beginning of the 21st century.

Oregon tugged at the nation when California was still unknown. The territory won the imagination of 19th-century America, which soon trampled Native American cultures in the rush for Willamette Valley land. In 1846, the Oregon Trail changed forever the destiny of the tribes and a young nation. In the years to come, the Oregon dream reinvented itself for new generations. During the Great Depression, the state lured busted farmers and laborers to the Bonneville Dam. In the 1940s, it drew African-Americans to the Portland shipyards. In the 1970s, it attracted hippies and

environmentalists. In the 1990s, it drew affluent Californians. They cashed out in Orange County or the Bay Area and came north to escape pollution and crime. They traveled in Mercedes sedans rather than Conestoga wagons, but they sought the same thing: Oregon's promise of a better life.

William Stafford, the late poet laureate of Oregon, explored the feelings the West provoked in one of his Methow Valley poems. It captures the way Oregon gripped newcomers.

> *These people look out and*
> *wonder. Is it magic? Is it*
> *the oceans of air off the Pacific?*
> *You can't*
> *walk through it without wrapping*
> *a new*
> *piece of tie around you, a readiness*
> *for a meadowlark,*
> *that brinkmanship a dawn can carry for*
> *lucky people all though the day.*

Freight wagons cross at Shaniko Flats in Wasco County. The federal law granting free land to whites helped prompt between 25,000 and 30,000 to migrate to Oregon between 1850 and 1855.

Today, the past lives in the "Far Corner," a place at once isolated from and inextricably bound to the American dream. This "progressive anachronism," as historian Gordon Dodds so aptly describes Oregon, has thrived and stumbled for nearly two centuries under the mantle of its awe-inspiring charter—not the document that framed a new territory, but the idea that lived in the minds of its people. In the 20th century, Oregon gained a progressive political reputation. The label was misleading; it obscured Oregon's wide cautious streak. Oregon was willing to be progressive—as with the environmental laws of the 1970s—only when it came to defending the old values. And those values were bound to the land like the gray, enveloping rain. Oregon: A place where the grass grew tall and green even in winter. Where the steady rain nurtured crops and family ambitions. A land of high mountains, salmon rivers, rich valleys where a family could acquire a square mile of paradise for the price of a 2,000-mile walk.

Of course, the dream didn't match the reality. But the gulf between myth and muddy winters didn't matter. What mattered was what people believed. Americans equated Oregon with a better life.

The intruders encountered an unfamiliar landscape. At least nine climate zones reached across a state larger than New England. Rainfall varied from 200 inches a year in the Coast Range near the headwaters of the Wilson River to 6 inches in the Alvord Desert, in the parched shadow of Steens Mountain.

Oregon was as geographically diverse as it would later be lacking in cultural variety. Eleven mountain ranges creased the state. The Columbia Gorge hid 71 waterfalls in a setting spectacular enough to make painter Albert Bierstadt blush. Gardeners grew palm trees in Curry County, while frost settled in the northeast mountains every month of the year. Winter buried the high Cascades under 70 feet of snow, while a weather anomaly created a "banana belt" on the south coast.

Newcomers were unprepared for the rich landscape. How they came to relate to the alpine forests and wild rivers forever defined what it meant to be an Oregonian.

"What makes Oregon different is how Oregonians relate to the land, to the place where they live," says Carl Abbott, a professor of urban studies at Portland State University. "And the place they relate to is not just their own city or town, it's the whole Northwest."

So what is the lesson of the past 150 years? Where does the Oregon story go from here? No doubt we will continue beating furiously, perhaps even progressively, into the past. Come what may, Oregon will define itself by this magnificent land form. Our fiercest political battles will be tied to the land. The Oregon dream will endure if Oregonians remember what we share instead of what divides us. The common ground is all around us: It is the love we have for this Oregon, this rare place, this idea.

Horse-drawn wagons travel along First Street, south of Morrison, near Hop Wo Washing and Ironing, sometime between 1850 and 1860.

BEYOND THE OREGON TRAIL 1850-1899

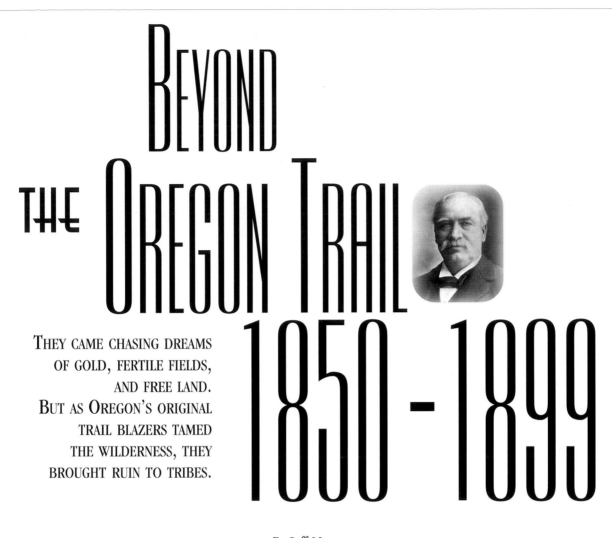

THEY CAME CHASING DREAMS OF GOLD, FERTILE FIELDS, AND FREE LAND. BUT AS OREGON'S ORIGINAL TRAIL BLAZERS TAMED THE WILDERNESS, THEY BROUGHT RUIN TO TRIBES.

By Jeff Mapes

The Oregon Trail Elementary School. Pioneer Mobile Home Park. Trail Dust Pizza. The announcer intoning, "And now, introducing your Portland Trail Blazers!" Yes, we are surrounded by the remembrances of our state's birth. Almost without realizing it, we have accumulated encrusted layers of mythology about visionary and supremely able pioneers who braved the hardships of the Oregon Trail to carve a new society from the wilderness. In truth, they were ordinary people who brought everyday hopes, dreams, and prejudices on their extraordinary journey. They fought over the character of the new state and grabbed for its abundant natural wealth. And as they created their society, they laid waste to an ancient one that had made the land its home. In just a few decades, with the aid of steel rails, abundant government subsidies, and powerful new technologies, they brought

A view of Portland's Skidmore Fountain looking south, circa 1880

large-scale logging, agriculture, and industry to the Northwest. Portland grew from a clearing in the woods into the West Coast's second-largest city, behind only San Francisco.

THE LURE OF GOLD AND A MILD CLIMATE

By 1850, the Oregon Territory was no longer a perplexing mystery to the citizens of that rapidly expanding republic, the United States of America. The explorers, trappers, and missionaries had spread word of the gentle climate and fertile soil, particularly in the Willamette Valley. Since 1843, a growing number of emigrants had worn a clear route for the Oregon Trail. In 1848, the federal government had brought territorial government to Oregon after settling a boundary dispute with Great Britain.

The discovery of gold in California turned the Oregon Trail into a virtual highway of dust and deep ruts as thousands jostled for the dream of easy riches. But in 1850, Congress also provided an enticing prize for emigrants to Oregon: free land. Along the trail, travelers had a camp song that encapsulated their hopes: "Come along, come along, don't be alarmed Uncle Sam is rich enough to give us all a farm."

Many of the would-be settlers came from the Mississippi and Missouri river valleys, escaping periodic flooding and contagious fevers. Some were in debt, some merely restless and looking for adventure. The simple pull of softer winters, year-round grazing, and abundant timber, fish, and game were as attractive then as the offer today of stock options to work at a dot-com.

"People didn't go out and do this as a great campaign for the nation," said Yale historian John Mack Faragher, one of the top scholars of the American West. "It came down to the practicalities of finding a better place to live."

The journey, which averaged just slightly more than four months in the 1850s, was certainly arduous, but the chief enemy is often forgotten today. It was disease, which killed about 10,000 travelers during the two decades of the trail's chief use. Cholera, normally an urban sickness, swept through the emigrants, who often found befouled water holes and encampments. "We could hardly walk for the cow dung," wrote Agnes Stewart of one creek-side camp in 1853, "and could hardly breathe for the smell of dead cattle."

The character and abilities of the emigrants varied widely. Some were well organized and carefully outfitted. But many took so much that they were forced to sell foodstuffs to lighten their over-burdened wagons. They were well armed but often inept with firearms. Accidental shootings were common, and the men often hunted just for sport, leaving rotting buffalo carcasses on the plains. In their later years, many of the pioneers glossed over all of this. Buttressed by an influential 1900 article by noted Oregon scientist Thomas Condon, the Oregon Pioneer Association promulgated the Darwinian idea that the emigrants were a self-selected elite perfectly matched to the rigors of the trail and the taming of the new territory.

The truth is more compelling. When whole families pushed and pulled their wagons over the daunting Blue Mountains of Eastern Oregon, it was the labor of people with whom we can identify. Their awe at the grandeur of the huge rock formations of the Western interior and their weariness with a journey that never seemed to end are emotions that still touch us.

"I would make a brave effort to be cheerful and patient until the camp work was done," wrote Lavinia Porter of her 1860 journey. "Then starting out ahead of the team and my men folks, when I thought I had gone beyond hearing distance, I would throw myself down on the unfriendly desert and give way like a child to sobs and tears, wishing myself back home with my friends and chiding myself for consenting to take this wild goose chase."

TRIBES BEFRIENDED, THEN ABUSED

Along the trail, emigrants and Native Americans often approached one another with a wary curiosity. What's often forgotten is that, particularly in the early years of the trail, the emigrants depended heavily on aid from Native Americans, who provided directions, helped them ford rivers, and traded with them. "If not for the Indians, a lot of [the emigrants] would not have survived on the trail," said Marjorie Waheneka, a National Park Service ranger on loan to the tribal museum on the Umatilla Indian Reservation, where she was born and reared.

As time wore on, and the numbers of emigrants multiplied, so did the conflicts. The would-be settlers didn't understand that their presence was bringing everything from disease to the disruption of tribal hunting grounds. Some whites considered the Native Americans to be barely human and bristled at Native American attempts to levy tolls. And a theft or

JOSEPH BUCHTEL
After arriving on the trail in 1852, Buchtel became Portland's chief photographer and by 1884 had more than 25,000 negatives of Oregon scenes and residents. He caught many of the firsts of Oregon—steamers, sawmills, fire engines—and its tragedies, such as the disastrous 1873 fire in downtown Portland. He also organized Portland's first baseball team in 1866, supervised the city's first fireboat, pushed for a bridge across the Willamette, and served as Multnomah County sheriff. While Buchtel was traveling in the 1880s, a partner decided to destroy thousands of files of his negatives.

intimidating behavior by an Native American led the emigrants to think the worst. One 1851 emigrant, suspecting that a Native American had stolen his horse, announced that he would kill the next Indian that he saw—and he did, shooting an unsuspecting man spearing a salmon in the Snake River. At times, Native Americans committed their own atrocities. In 1854, just east of Fort Boise, another encounter over the theft of a horse turned into a pitched battle that left 19 emigrants of the Ward party dead and, in some instances, shockingly mutilated.

The late historian John D. Unruh, whose 1979 book, *The Plains Across,* is the best scholarly work about the trail, concluded that about 360 whites and nearly 430 Native Americans were killed in violence against each other on the trail in the 1840s and 1850s. White marauders disguised as Native Americans also ratcheted up the violence by preying on emigrants. In addition, Unruh said, newspapers of the era fanned hatred and fear against the Native Americans by printing secondhand accounts of massacres that never occurred. And each act of violence, real or imagined, spawned fervent editorializing in favor of military reprisals. Thomas Dryer, founding editor of *The Oregonian*, was among the most vituperative, describing extermination as one course of action for "these worthless races resembling the human form."

Just the coming of the whites—and their illnesses—already had weakened the tribes of the Northwest. A malaria epidemic in 1830-33 swept through the region and decimated villages. Disease also lay behind the infamous 1847 killings at the Whitman Mission that sparked warfare with the Cayuse. Native American hotheads, inflamed by rumors that their family members were dying not from a measles epidemic but by deliberate poisoning, slaughtered 14 missionaries. The war ended in Oregon City in 1850 with the trial, conviction, and public hanging of five Cayuse men, despite serious questions about the guilt of three of them.

FREE LAND TOUCHES OFF BOOM

The most momentous event of 1850—for Native Americans and whites alike—took place in Washington, D.C., when Congress passed the Oregon Donation Land Act. It provided as much as 320 acres to white male settlers, depending on when they had settled in the territory. And if the man was married, his wife could receive a like amount. This

The Shaniko Stage arrives in Madras, circa late 1880s.

act intensified the rush for Oregon land and produced a marriage boom that, given the predominance of men among the frontier population, often turned children into brides. Esther M. Selover Lockhart, a well-educated Yankee who came to Oregon in 1851, wrote of a visit to the home of a man who was 28, and his wife, 11: "She helped her husband prepare the supper for their guests, but after the meal was finished, she disappeared," Lockhart wrote. "Finally she was found in the back yard, having a glorious time with a neighbor's little girl, 'teetering' on a board thrown over a log. The husband came back in the house, cleared the table, and washed the dishes, remarking as he did so, 'Lizzie's young yet!'"

For the Native Americans, the land act was a betrayal. The 1848 law creating the territory preserved tribal land claims pending their resolution by treaty. But the 1850 act—the handiwork of Oregon's first delegate to Congress, Samuel Thurston, who wanted all Native Americans moved east of the Cascades—opened lands throughout the Oregon Territory for white settlement. It was the first time the federal government gave away free land.

BLOODSHED AND BANISHMENT

It was not free land, however, but a big gold strike on the Rogue River in 1852 that caused the worst violence in Oregon. As miners and settlers piled into Southern Oregon, they drove Native

JOHN C. AINSWORTH After gold lured him to California in 1850, he came to Oregon and founded a mercantile business in Oregon City. But his past work on a Mississippi steamboat had sparked an interest in shipping. He formed Oregon Steam Navigation Company in 1860 and was engaged in river and rail activities for 30 years. The company operated a monopoly on the Columbia River for years. In 1880, he sold his shipping interests and went into banking, organizing Ainsworth National Bank of Portland.

Americans from the gravel beds that had been their villages and destroyed their usual food sources. Many of the Native Americans didn't go quietly, and they launched their own attacks. Dozens of whites organized themselves into volunteer militias that indiscriminately attacked and killed Native Americans, regardless of whether they were peaceful.

One group of volunteers, 441 strong, even billed the government $107,287, and included such fanciful expenses as 29,100 candles and 19,000 bars of soap. "War was more profitable than gold mining!" historian Stephen Beckham noted in his book about the Rogue River wars, *Requiem for a People*.

The fighting finally ended in 1856 and the surviving Native Americans were sent to two newly created reservations: the Siletz on the coast and the Grand Ronde in the Willamette Valley. Both were the handiwork of Joel Palmer, who played an influential role as the Oregon territory's superintendent of Indian affairs from 1853–56. A humane man, Palmer wanted to protect Native Americans from the "pestiferous influence of degraded white men" by isolating them on reservations.

Two of the early national crusaders for Native American rights did come from Oregon. Englishman John Beeson, who had settled in the Rogue Valley in 1853, spoke out against the treatment of Native Americans and, as a result, felt forced to flee Oregon to avoid a lynch mob. He wrote "A Plea for the Indians" and lectured around the country. Alfred

OREGON
LIFE FROM
1850-1899

PEOPLE

In 1860, white men between ages 20 and 29 out-number women more than 2 to 1.

The Chinese population is 3,330 in 1870, fewer than 100 of them women.

WORK

In 1860, 309 manufacturers employ 968 men and 10 women; by 1900, 3,088 employ 15,120 men, 1,821 women, and 295 children.

In 1880, Oregon Railway & Navigation Company advertises for laborers at $1.75 a day.

In 1860, Oregon has 5,657 farms; by 1900, 35,837.

HOME

In 1850, dried apples sell for 75 cents a pound, eggs for 50 cents a dozen, and salt for $6 for 100 pounds.

In 1889, a good cottage on a 28-by-100-foot lot in Southeast Portland sells for $2,600, and a 104-acre farm a mile from Gervais in Marion County sells for $6,000.

PLAY

The first state fair is held in 1861 in what is now Gladstone; the fair moves to Salem the following year.

In 1864, Portland's first lending library opens with 1,400 books purchased with $2,500 gathered from door-to-door canvassing.

The Pioneer Baseball Club of East Portland forms in 1866; several Oregon towns soon boast their own teams. Sunday games, however, are discouraged as immoral.

GETTING AROUND

Bicyclists are credited with starting the crusade for better roads in 1890s.

A horse-drawn streetcar system forms in Portland in 1871.

In 1893, the East Side Railway Company begins electric streetcar service from Portland to Oregon City; the trip takes one hour.

RELIGION AND VALUES

In 1860, Oregon has 75 churches.

River View Cemetery is established in 1882 and is open to all races and creeds.

ENVIRONMENT

Portland takes ownership of a privately collected group of no-longer-wanted pet bears, parakeets, and the like to form a public zoo in 1887 (the beginnings of the Oregon Zoo).

One of the first timber conservation efforts begins in 1891 when Congress grants the president the power to establish forest reserves.

An investigation by *The Oregonian* in 1887 concludes that the Columbia River is being fished out, labeling the situation an "emergency."

SCHOOL

The first free public school in Portland opens in 1851; John T. Outhouse was the teacher. Amid opposition, Oregon's first public high school opens in Portland in 1869 with an enrollment of 45 students. By 1880 enrollment reaches only 140.

The Chemawa Indian School opens in Salem in 1886 with 207 students; its forerunner was in Forest Grove.

WAR

In the Rogue River wars of 1851 to 1856, losses of whites were "probably less than 200 for the entire duration" with a "slightly higher Indian loss."

The Trail of Tears starts in 1856 when the government rounds up 300 to 400 members of 22 tribes west of the Cascades and herds them to the Grand Ronde and Siletz reservations.

The Union Army begins construction of Fort Stevens in 1863 to guard the Columbia River against Confederate raiders.

CRIME AND JUSTICE

The first state penitentiary is located in Portland in 1851; moved to Salem in 1866.

Charity Lamb becomes the first woman convicted of murder for the 1854 ax slaying of her husband. She serves several years of hard labor at the Portland city jail and frequently is seen doing the warden's family washing.

POLITICS AND LAW

In 1862, Oregon adopts a law requiring all residents of color to pay an annual tax of $5. If they could not pay the tax, the state could force them into service maintaining state roads for 50 cents a day.

Meacham, another former Indian superintendent who had played an unsuccessful peacemaker role in the Modoc War of 1872–73, toured the nation with Frank Riddle, who was white, and his Modoc wife, Toby, who came to be known as Winema. Meacham and Beeson both spoke in favor of preserving traditional tribal cultures. But federal policy by then was clear: The Native Americans should join white society and forget their past.

In the early years of the Siletz and the Grand Ronde reservations, Native Americans fared poorly. Misguided attempts to farm on the Siletz, which once stretched for 125 miles along the coast, repeatedly failed, and mortality was high. Both reservations were steadily whittled in size as whites found that the land had economic value. Chief John of the Rogues was once famously reputed to have said, "It is not your wars but your peace that kills my people."

One of the last of the wars between whites and Native Americans in Oregon came to tug at the nation's conscience. The Nez Perce had been ordered out of their traditional home in the Wallowa Valley despite an 1876 government report upholding their treaty rights to stay. As they prepared to leave in June of 1877, a group of young Nez Perce men sought vengeance on their white tormentors and killed 18 settlers. Properly handled by the authorities, the violence could have been contained. But Army officers saw it as the beginning of all-out war. The Nez Perce, led by Chief Joseph, fled on a 1,300-mile retreat through the mountains of Idaho, Wyoming, and Montana as they repeatedly outmaneuvered the Army troops pursuing them. Finally, they surrendered four months later and were sent to Kansas.

For once, the sympathy of many white Americans was with the Native Americans, particularly after newspapers began reporting about the Nez Perces' abysmal living conditions. Six years later, they were allowed to move to reservations in Idaho and Washington. Chief Joseph visited the Wallowa Valley in 1899 and 1900, but local settlers rebuffed his pleas to buy a tract of land.

Portland writer Terence O'Donnell proclaimed in his biography of Joel Palmer that Oregon history has been generally a "summer's afternoon spent on the banks of a pretty river." Except, he added, for the Indian wars, "those thirty years of butchery that bloodied, and stained for good, our beginnings."

HENRY PITTOCK
Pittock arrived in Oregon "penniless and barefoot" in 1853. At first he supported himself by helping build a log cabin and splitting fence rails. But he soon got a job as a typesetter at *The Oregonian*. By 1860, he took over ownership in lieu of back wages, launching an empire that would incorporate real estate, banking, railroads, sheep ranching, steamboats, silver mining, and the pulp and paper industry. Despite claims by *The Oregonian*'s first editor, Thomas Dryer, Pittock is regarded as among the first party to reach Mount Hood's summit. On one of his many climbs, someone suggested they sit down and rest. Pittock responded, "The man who sits down never reaches the top."

DIVIDED BY THE STATEHOOD DEBATE

Although it didn't involve bloodshed, the quarreling over statehood for Oregon didn't seem like a summer's afternoon. In fact, it took the entire decade of the 1850s, with voters thrice rejecting resolutions calling for a constitutional convention. In large part, the delay was caused by the virulent political splits in the growing territory. The "Salem clique," allied with the Democratic Party, held the upper hand in state politics. But the Whigs, the forerunners to the Republican Party, won favor among Portland businessmen. By the middle of the decade, the anti-Catholic, anti-immigrant "Know Nothing" party (so-called for the secrecy pledges among members) also had taken root in Oregon.

The growing national debate about slavery complicated matters. Although few settlers wanted to bring slavery to Oregon, many sympathized with the South. But once the Supreme Court ruled in its 1857 Dred Scott decision that a territory couldn't ban slavery, the deadlock was broken.

A constitutional convention was called quickly, and the voters approved the new framework for a state government. They also voted strongly to prohibit slavery—but they voted even more overwhelmingly to exclude "free Negroes" from Oregon. Most settlers clearly wanted to stay as far away as possible from the conflicts surrounding slavery—and they just as clearly saw this new Eden as one for whites only. The state's small African-American population faced Southern-style segregation that lasted well into the 20th century. Chinese immigrants who began moving to Oregon also faced an unfriendly reception and, in the 1880s, were driven by mobs out of Oregon City, Mount Tabor, and Albina.

As the Civil War loomed, it took more than a year for Congress to approve Oregon's statehood legislation, which President James Buchanan signed into law on February 14, 1859. Lost in the debate about slavery was the strong bias against industry and big business in the new state's constitution.

"We have an agricultural community . . . and there is where you look for the true and solid wealth and happiness of a people," explained Judge Matthew Deady, who presided over the constitutional convention. "In the manufacturing countries, power, political and otherwise, is in the hands of capitalists; there are many people dependent on them, and dependence begets servility."

1850-1859

1850: Congress enacts the Oregon Donation Land Act, prompting 25,000 to 30,000 to migrate before the act expires in 1855. *The Oregonian* begins publication in Portland on December 4. Mail service between San Francisco and the Columbia River begins.

1851: Portland incorporates. Lawmakers move the state capital to Salem. *The Oregon Statesman* begins publication in Oregon City, then moves to Salem.

1853: The Washington Territory separates from Oregon. The Rogue River Indian wars begin and will continue to 1856. The Typographical Society is the first labor union in Oregon.

1854: The first Capitol is built in Salem at a cost of $40,000.

1855: The Yakima Indian War begins.

1856: Parts of Eastern Washington and Oregon are closed to settlers by Army order, because of the Indian war.

1857: Meier & Frank Company opens in Portland.

1858: Oregon holds its first election of state officers.

1859: On February 14, Congress grants statehood; Oregon becomes 33rd star on the American flag.

1860-1869

1860: Captain John C. Ainsworth organizes Oregon Steam Navigation Company.

1861: The first Oregon State Fair is held near Oregon City, in what is now Gladstone.

1862: The Oregon Pony provides the state's first steam-driven rail service, between Bonneville and Cascade Locks.

1863: The state's first telegraph line links Portland and Salem.

1864: The first salmon cannery opens in Astoria. A telegraph line connects Portland and San Francisco.

1865: Henry Weinhard moves brewery to Portland.

1867: Oregon Iron Company in Lake Oswego is the first iron smelter west of the Rockies.

1868: Corvallis College, now Oregon State University, is the first state-supported higher-education institution.

1869: Construction begins on Federal (Pioneer) Courthouse. Asahel Bush and W. S. Ladd open the Ladd & Bush Bank in Salem.

1870-1879

1871: Portland Street Railway Company incorporates.

1872: The Modoc Indian War rages.

1873: The cornerstone is laid for a second Capitol in Salem.

1875: Good Samaritan and St. Vincent hospitals and the New Market Theatre open.

1876: The University of Oregon opens in Eugene.

1877: The Nez Perce Tribe and the U.S. Army clash in Northeast Oregon; Chief Joseph and his people flee their Wallowa homeland, pursued by troops.

1878: Pacific Northwest Bell begins service in Portland. The Bannock Indian War flares.

1880-1889

1882: The Old Church is built at Southwest 11th and Clay.

1883: Direct rail service begins between Portland and the Eastern United States; the first Northern Pacific train steams into Portland.

1886: Portland Coca-Cola Bottling Company begins operations.

1887: The Morrison Street Bridge opens, the first bridge to span the Willamette.

1889: Portland General Electric Company begins service. Willamette Falls Electric Company sends power to Portland, the first long-distance transmission in the nation.

1890-1899

1890: Union Station opens.

1891: The Madison Street (Hawthorne) Bridge is finished.

1892: The Portland Art Association organizes. Jake's Restaurant opens.

1893: The University of Oregon and Albany College meet in the state's first football game; UO wins 44-2. "The Great Flood" sends the Columbia and Willamette Rivers well beyond their banks.

1895: *The New Age*, Oregon's first African-American newspaper, begins publication.

1898: Battleship *Oregon* steams out of Puget Sound, bound for climactic battle of Spanish-American War.

1899: The State Legislature creates boards of examiners for teachers and barbers.

But economic forces much larger than that of the pioneer farmer were quick to assert their primacy. Just one year after statehood, steamer captain John C. Ainsworth headed a group that formed Oregon Steam Navigation Company, which enjoyed a monopoly on freight and passenger traffic on the Columbia and moved into the railroad business as well. During the next 40 years, the company and its successors would be a key pawn in the byzantine battles that shaped railroad development in the Northwest. One business titan after another would vie for control of the steel rails that brought industry and economic growth.

Ben Holladay, a swashbuckling stagecoach magnate from San Francisco, was the first serious challenger to Ainsworth and the buttoned-down Portland merchants. Holladay based his operations on the east side of Portland and—proclaiming that he'd turn the west side into a "rat hole"—beat out the locals in the race to win approval from the Oregon Legislature to build a railroad to California. Holladay did it by showering the legislators with drink, women, and, reputedly, outright bribes. For many legislators, it was their first taste of champagne—but not their last. By the 1890s, the Oregon Legislature was regarded as corrupt as any in the nation. It helped spark the populism that produced the political reforms of the first two decades of the 20th century. Holladay, however, never finished his railroad to California after his empire collapsed in the financial panic of 1873.

The next significant railroad figure was an unlikely one. Henry Villard, a journalist turned financier, came to Oregon in 1873 to represent the interests of German bondholders (who, having found the Franco–Prussian War good for business, had a lot to lend). Villard eventually took control of Oregon Steam Navigation and used it to form Oregon Railway & Navigation Company. At first, he wanted to connect his new railroad with the Union Pacific—one-half of the partnership that built the nation's first transcontinental route. But Villard soon realized he might face ruinous competition from the Northern Pacific, which had been promised lavish land grants from Congress for completion of a rail link between the Northwest and the East.

In 1881, Villard audaciously organized a "blind pool" to raise $8 million from trusting investors, and he used the money to secretly buy up stock in

Above: *A train pulls into the station in La Grande in the 1880s. Oregon Railway & Navigation Company was a key link in the development of a northern transcontinental line.* Right: *A family poses with early lumber tools in Tillamook County, circa 1880.* Far right: *Downtown Portland during a flood in 1876.*

Northern Pacific. Once he seized control, Villard pushed hard to complete Oregon's first transcontinental link. When the first westbound train arrived in Portland on September 11, 1883, it was the "greatest display ever witnessed in this city," proclaimed *The Oregonian*. It also represented Villard's downfall. He had failed to keep his costs in line, and the often shoddily built railroad traversed long miles of empty territory that produced little freight. James J. Hill, a St. Paul, Minnesota, magnate as hardheaded about railroading as Villard was visionary, soon assumed control of the Northern Pacific.

But the other part of Villard's empire, the Oregon Railway Company, eventually found its way into the hands of Edward Harriman's Union Pacific. As the century came to a close, Hill built his own rail link to Seattle and battled Harriman for dominance in the Northwest. Hill's most lasting influence on the region, however, revolved around his conversations with his next-door neighbor in St. Paul, Frederick Weyerhaeuser. Hill told the timber baron of the immense forests of the Northwest and the railroad's 38.6 million acres of land grants. Weyerhaeuser, near to exhausting the old-growth forests of the Upper Midwest, was intrigued. On January 3, 1900, the two completed their deal. In the largest private land purchase in U.S. history to that point, Weyerhaeuser and his partners bought 900,000 acres of prime Washington timberland for $6 an acre.

It was the start of a new empire at the end of the Oregon Trail.

Flora Dora girls perform in Northwest Portland at the 1905 Lewis and Clark Exposition, the largest production in Oregon's history.

HIGH HOPES IN THE 1900s

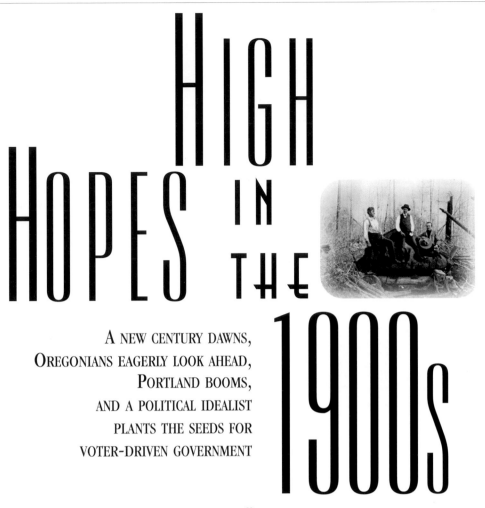

A NEW CENTURY DAWNS,
OREGONIANS EAGERLY LOOK AHEAD,
PORTLAND BOOMS,
AND A POLITICAL IDEALIST
PLANTS THE SEEDS FOR
VOTER-DRIVEN GOVERNMENT

By Jeff Mapes

If you live in Oregon, you've probably met somebody like this. He grew up in the Midwest and tried a stolid professional career but left the life of an Organization Man. He drifted west and, at the age of 30, landed penniless and sickly on a Clackamas County farm that was part fruit orchard, part intellectual salon. In such environs, he quickly became seized by an idea he was convinced would make Oregon an even more perfect Eden.

This, in short, is the beginning of the story of William Simon U'Ren, who, around the turn of the century, launched the most powerful political reforms Oregon has ever seen. Many of his ideas took root throughout the nation. And his belief that the average person can move a society toward perfection has become deeply ingrained in the Oregon psyche.

A horse-drawn float parades at the first official Portland Rose Festival in 1907. Seeds of the annual celebration were planted at the 1905 Portland Rose Carnival and other, earlier rose events, including the creation of the Portland Rose Society, now the nation's oldest, in 1888.

U'Ren, a slight, soft-spoken son of a long line of English blacksmiths, fathered the initiative and referendum system approved by Oregon voters in 1902. To break the power of the political bosses who once held sway in Oregon, U'Ren and his allies also created the direct election of U.S. senators, the direct presidential primary, tougher conflict-of-interest laws, and the right to recall public officials. None of these reforms ever resulted in the Utopian society that U'Ren envisioned. But U'Ren produced a wave that has rippled down to the present.

After an initial burst of reform in Oregon, the initiative system lay largely quiet for decades, only to reassert itself with a vengeance in the 1990s to once again reshape the state and its government. Here, for better or worse, the voters rule, thanks to U'Ren. No politician will ever become too powerful, no big economic interest will go unchallenged. And, it seems, no popular idea, fad or code of conduct will fail to be tested at the polls. Thanks to U'Ren's evangelism, the initiative spread to two dozen states, including, most importantly, our huge neighbor to the south, California. It forever established in the national mind that Oregon was, as the *Almanac of American Politics* put it, "an experimental commonwealth and laboratory of reform on the Pacific Rim."

WILLIAM SIMON U'REN The father of the state's initiative and referendum system, U'Ren once was called the "lawgiver" for his promotion of these and other political reforms that reverberated throughout the nation.

A TIME OF GREAT CHANGE

As is true now, the beginning of the new century was a time of incredible economic dynamism and rapid technological and social change. In just a generation, the railroads had expanded their reach throughout Oregon, bringing the promise of settlement to almost every corner of the state. Steam power and other innovations spawned a massive, efficient timber industry that brought with it huge fortunes and equally gigantic changes in the landscape.

And in the middle of it all was Portland, suddenly a booming metropolis, rivaled in the West only by San Francisco and Denver and a new upstart up north, Seattle.

A dense streetcar network lifted Portlanders above the mud that encircled the city, a liquid version of the sands that surround a desert oasis. A warren of solid office buildings, ramshackle boarding houses, prosperous storefronts, and saloons, saloons, saloons spread from the waterfront. There was a Chinese community that endured periodic waves of anti-Asian hysteria and a smaller African-American community that faced Southern-type segregation and racial exclusion laws.

Above: *Portland's buildings were only beginning to sprout above trees and the city's eastside was largely undeveloped in this 1903 panorama from the hills west of downtown.* Left: *By 1905, Portland had a well-developed streetcar network as shown in this view looking east on Southwest Morrison Street from Third Avenue.*

Above it all, the new wealth was displayed in fine mansions designed to mimic what you could find in London or New York. Across the river, spanned by an ever-growing number of bridges, developers laid one suburban tract after another.

And the corruption and the financial shenanigans that accompanied this development were oh-so-sophisticated.

WAVES OF SETTLERS ARRIVE

The movers and shakers were so confident of Portland's status as a big-league city that they decided to assert their primacy by bringing a world's fair to town, the equivalent today of hosting the Olympics. The Lewis and Clark Exposition of 1905 was the biggest production in Oregon history, never to be equaled.

The Oregonians of 1900 thought they were literally creating a new society. Less than 100 years before, Meriwether Lewis and William Clark had reached the mouth of the Columbia River, the westernmost point of a journey through a region as exotic to the citizens of the new republic of the United States as a *Star Trek* episode is to us now.

Portland, incorporated in 1851, was the City that Gravity Built. From their advantageous point at the confluence of the Columbia and the Willamette, the early merchants became the brokers of the growing trade in agriculture and timber. Portland merchants prospered by supplying the risk-takers of the Western gold rushes and the military in the Spanish-American War of 1898. They helped establish the character of a city that appreciated prosperity but also tended to go for the sure thing over the big gamble. As Portland historian E. Kimbark MacColl put it, the city has always liked to travel first class on a steerage ticket.

WHEAT AND TIMBER FUEL THE ECONOMY

In the first decade of the 1900s, Oregon's population grew by nearly two-thirds as the state's economy took off once again. Wheat was the main crop, while timber barons such as Simon Benson pioneered the technology used to wrest trees from remote hillsides. It was a muscular world that

Left: *The Lewis and Clark Exposition drew more than 3 million paid admissions in 1905. From the Grand Staircase, fairgoers got a view of the government building on the site, which today is the Guild's Lake industrial district of Northwest Portland.* Below: *Horses and nets catch salmon on the Columbia River near Astoria, circa 1900. The abundance of fishing helped make Astoria Oregon's second-largest city in 1900.*

Floodwaters and a dam failure on Willow Creek in 1903 led to 250 deaths in Heppner and destroyed the city.

produced awe-inspiring sights. In Hood River, for example, the Stanley Smith Lumber Company built the world's only level log flume, a huge network of trip gates, holding ponds, and sluice flumes that stretched for six miles.

Benson developed huge log rafts, 1,000 feet long and shaped like cigars, that his crews towed to California. The first contained enough wood to build a complete sawmill in San Diego. It was Oregon lumber that helped rebuild San Francisco after the 1906 earthquake and fires.

As U'Ren began to pursue his reforms, a few powerful interests ruled Oregon. By the early 1900s, the Harriman and Hill railroad empires held sway in the Northwest, and the Portland Railway Light & Power Company, the forerunner of Portland General Electric, controlled the city's streetcar and utility network. The banks, the timber companies, and even the saloon owners were parts of a powerful machine that controlled the dominant Republican Party and the levers of local and state government.

MacColl, who wrote a trilogy exploring the growth of Portland's power structure, gleaned one small example of how this domination cheated residents. In 1900, for taxation purposes, Oregon assessed railroad property at $3,285 per mile— less than half the $7,427 in Washington and the $9,719 in California.

No one personified political corruption better than John Mitchell, who spent 22 years as a U.S. senator from Oregon while serving as a legal counsel for railroad entities. Mitchell could be blunt about his loyalties. Referring to Ben Holladay, an

C. S. SAMUEL JACKSON
He took a 4-month-old struggling daily newspaper in July 1902, changed its name from the *Evening Journal* to the *Oregon Daily Journal*, and revived it. Jackson had been the editor of the *East Oregonian* for two decades in Pendleton, but his first job there was as a stagecoach agent.

early Oregon railroad magnate, Mitchell said, "Ben Holladay's politics are my politics, and what Ben Holladay wants I want."

Still, Mitchell, whose reputation had been soured by the exposure of a tangled sexual past that included bigamy, didn't worry overly about public opinion. He served in the days when senators were chosen by state legislators, who were all too often up for bid. Ironically, though, it was Mitchell who gave U'Ren the opening to bring the initiative to Oregon.

SUPPORT BUILDS FOR REFORMS

U'Ren, who had trained as a lawyer in Denver and came to detest the political corruption there, learned of the idea from a book about Switzerland's "direct legislation" when he lived with Seth and Sophronia Lewelling on their farm near Milwaukie. The Lewellings were more than just orchardists. They opened their home to a wide circle of freethinkers, who ranged from famous suffragist Susan B. Anthony to spiritualists who conducted séances.

U'Ren became a key figure in Oregon's Populist movement and made the initiative an important political issue. In 1896, he was elected to his only public office, a two-year term in the Oregon House. U'Ren arrived in Salem for the 1897 session, which turned out to be the most infamous in Oregon history. Mitchell sided with gold backers over those who also wanted to use silver as a monetary standard. At the time, it was a life-and-death struggle. Would the

OREGON LIFE IN THE 1900s

PEOPLE

Portland, the state's largest city, is the nation's 42nd largest with 90,426 residents in 1900; Astoria is the state's second-largest city, with 8,381 residents.

256,125 Oregonians are U.S.-born of native parentage; 84,596 are U.S.-born of parents born in a foreign country; 9,367 of those born in another country are from China; Native American population numbers 4,063.

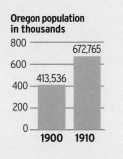

Population boom

Oregon's population exploded, particularly in Portland. The city, which accounted for only one-tenth of the state's population in 1880, accounted for one-third by 1910.

Source: U.S. Census Bureau

Oregon population in thousands

1900	1910
413,536	672,765

WORK

35,837 farms, covering slightly more than 10 million acres, compared with 34,030 farms covering 17.5 million acres today.

3,088 manufacturers, employing 17,236; 1,821 are women, and 295 are children younger than 16.

HOME

A five-room cottage on a 50-by-125-foot lot in Albina goes for $1,250.

Good, clean rice sells for $1 for 25 pounds, graham flour at 15 cents for a 10-pound bag, and a pound of Hoffman House Java and Mocha Coffee for 30 cents.

A chamber pot sells for $2, children's drawers for 25 cents; men's suits are advertised from $10 to $30; a Roadwagon Runabout (horse) buggy sells for $60.

PLAY

Oaks Park, now one of America's oldest amusement parks, opens in 1905.

The Fisherman's Bride is the first movie filmed in Oregon, made in Astoria in 1908.

Uncle Tom's Cabin breaks all records with a matinee at Cordray's Theater, with 1,700 women and children attending in May 1908 and more than 300 turned away.

F. Bruckman of Portland invents an ice-cream cone rolling machine that produces leak-proof cones.

GETTING AROUND

By 1906, Portland boasts 28 electric streetcar lines and interurbans.

Oregon registers 218 licensed automobiles by 1905.

ENVIRONMENT

The Columbia white-tailed deer, mountain goats, and coastal sea otters have virtually disappeared because of hunting and loss of habitat.

Coastal rivers yield 1.4 million wild coho in 1900, compared with fewer than 100,000 in 1997.

SCHOOL

89,405 pupils in public schools attend an average 84 days in 1900.

WAR

1,630 Oregonians fight in the Spanish-American War and subsequent Philippine Insurrection; 65 die, most of disease.

NATIONAL FIRSTS

In 1904, Oregon becomes the first state to vote on a citizen initiative.

In 1908, Lola Baldwin becomes the nation's first Civil Service policewoman.

CRIME AND JUSTICE

After a 1903 Portland execution draws 3,000 onlookers, the Legislature assigns all future executions to take place in state prison.

In 1908, the U.S. Supreme Court upholds Muller vs. Oregon, which recognizes "inherent differences" between men and women that justify a law setting a maximum 10-hour work day for women.

Timber workers in Tillamook County, circa 1900, are shown with a steam donkey, one of the new items of technology that helped revolutionize logging and expand its reach. The equipment was used to pull logs out of the woods. Portland became the nation's No. 1 lumber-producing city in 1905.

business establishment protect its assets by a tight money standard (gold), or would an inflated money supply (backed also by silver, the popular position in Oregon) ease the plight of hard-pressed farmers?

U'Ren had first offered to support Mitchell's reelection as senator if he would support the initiative. When that dance with the devil didn't work, U'Ren allied himself with the free-silver crowd, in particular Jonathan S. Bourne, a rich, cynical scion of a wealthy Massachusetts family who had his own silver mines near Baker City. Bourne agreed to support U'Ren's reform package. Together, the two played a leading role in preventing the Legislature from organizing by making sure there weren't enough legislators for a quorum. It involved unsavory politicking on the part of U'Ren, who denied accusations he had been on the take.

And so the "hold-up" session passed into history without passing any bills and without sending Mitchell back to the U.S. Senate. Most important for U'Ren, with Bourne's help, he now had the political clout to pass the initiative through the 1899 and 1901 sessions, a requirement then for constitutional

HARVEY SCOTT
The powerful editor of *The Oregonian* from 1865 to 1910, Scott was a shrewd businessman and a fervent editorialist who had his own political ambitions. He unsuccessfully maneuvered to become Theodore Roosevelt's vice presidential nominee in 1904.

amendments. By the time it reached the voters in 1902, U'Ren's reform had become an idea almost beyond reproach, and it passed by a ratio of more than 10 to 1.

TIMBER SCANDAL HITS OREGON

Of course, political life in Oregon didn't immediately change. Mitchell had bullied his way back to the Senate in 1901. His real Waterloo came when he was caught in the middle of the timber fraud trials that began in 1904. For years, a law reserving public timberlands for small settlers in 160-acre chunks had been routinely ignored. Big operators used front men and other schemes, with help from corrupt officials, to amass large landholdings. Lands meant to be under the control of the state for the benefit of schools also found their way to private ownership.

President Theodore Roosevelt sent special prosecutor Francis J. Heney to Oregon to clean house. He returned with a spectacular haul: 33 convictions, including those of Mitchell,

Congressman John N. Williamson, U.S. Attorney John Hall, a couple of state senators, and the former U.S. deputy surveyor. Stephen Puter, a wheeler-dealer who played a central role in the timber frauds, turned against his fellow conspirators and wrote the sensational exposé *Looters of the Public Domain.*

"Thousands upon thousands of acres, which included the very cream of timber claims in Oregon and Washington, were secured by Eastern lumber-men and capitalists," he wrote from his cell in the Multnomah County jail, ". . . and nearly all of the claims, to my certain knowledge, were fraudulently obtained."

Despite the convictions, Puter complained the timber barons got off unscathed.

Mitchell, fighting to keep his Senate seat and overturn his bribery and perjury convictions, didn't last long. In 1905, he bled to death after visiting a dentist to have four teeth extracted.

Roosevelt continued to battle the Western timber industry, which all too often operated under the philosophy of cut and run. With the help of his

GEORGE HARDIN
He walked the beat on the east side and drove Portland's horse-drawn police wagon in the 1900s, making him the city's first African-American officer, even though state laws excluded or severely restricted African-Americans. Hardin became a sheriff's deputy in 1915.

influential forest chief, Gifford Pinchot, Roosevelt had placed 150 million acres into protected reserves over the howls of the industry.

In 1907, Oregon Senator Charles Fulton attempted to stop Roosevelt by tacking a rider to an appropriations bill, which the president couldn't afford to veto, specifying that no new reserves could be added in Oregon and five other Western states. Before Roosevelt signed the bill, however, Pinchot and his staff burned the midnight oil preparing proclamations allowing the president to lock up another 16 million acres of reserves in the West.

REFORMS SPREAD

Reform came to the local level in the person of Harry Lane, a physician who battled both vice and the trusts with equal fervor as Portland mayor from 1905 to 1909. With a large unattached male popula-tion, thanks to the steamships, railroads, and timber camps, Portland was a hotbed of prostitution, drink, and gambling. While Lane tried to shut down the

NEWSREEL

1900

Oregon voters reject granting women the right to vote, the first of three rejections in the decade. Elk Fountain is installed in downtown Portland at a cost of $20,000. The Afro-American League organizes in Portland. The Atiyeh brothers open a carpet store.

1901

The Oregon Legislature endorses the idea of a Lewis and Clark Exposition. The *Evening Journal* debuts in Portland; soon renamed the *Oregon Daily Journal*. The University of Portland is founded.

1902

Voters adopt the constitutional right to accept or reject laws passed by the Legislature and to initiate laws through petition. The Willamette Meteorite is discovered near West Linn. Congress establishes Crater Lake National Park. Counties gain the right to ban alcoholic beverages.

1903

A flash flood and a dam failure on Willow Creek kill 250 people in Heppner. President Theodore Roosevelt lays the cornerstone of the Lewis and Clark monument in Washington Park. The state publishes its first Voters' Pamphlet. Portland Railway Company opens the Alberta Line. McCants Stewart of Portland is admitted to the Oregon State Bar and becomes the state's first African-American attorney. The *Advocate*, an African-American-owned newspaper, begins publication in Portland.

1904

Timber fraud trials start and will lead to 33 convictions, including that of U.S. Senator John Mitchell. Chief Joseph of the Nez Perce dies at age 67. Albina Engine & Machine Works goes into business. Portland Manufacturing Co., a St. Johns box and barrel factory owned by the Autzen family, produces the nation's first commercial plywood. A 1902 steam locomobile chugs across the Coast Range into Tillamook.

1905

The Lewis and Clark Exposition draws 3,040,000 paid admissions during five months in Northwest Portland. The State Library opens in Salem. Portland becomes the nation's No. 1 lumber-manufacturing city by cutting 541 million board feet. The Albertina Kerr Nursery opens. Blitz Weinhard Company forms. The new $400,000 Morrison Street Bridge opens. Portland Mayor George H. Williams is indicted for refusing to perform duties; however, the charge is later dismissed.

1906

Portland Railway Light & Power Company is sold to Eastern interests. Governor George Chamberlain wins reelection. He will be the last Democrat to win two terms until John Kitzhaber in the 1990s. The Oregon Electric Railway Company incorporates. Portland Automobile Club organizes as the city raises the speed limit from 8 mph to 10 mph.

1907

The Portland Rose Festival Association incorporates and produces the first official Rose Festival. Carrie Lee Chamberlain, daughter of Governor Chamberlain, is named "Queen Flora." A nationwide panic prompts a state bank holiday, and the Legislature creates corporation and banking divisions.

1908

Voters approve a corrupt-practices act and the right of voters to recall public officials. Fairview Training Center opens in Salem. President Roosevelt establishes the Malheur National Wildlife Refuge. Burlington Northern Railroad incorporates in Portland. Benson High School opens.

1909

President William Howard Taft creates the Oregon Caves National Monument. Pendleton Woolen Mills starts in Portland. Construction begins on the Pittock Mansion. The Kenton Hotel opens in North Portland. The first attempt at airplane flight in Salem ends in a crash.

The 16-ton Willamette Meteorite was found in 1902 in a field south of Portland. Today, Oregon's Confederated Tribes of Grand Ronde are seeking ownership of the meteorite, which is at the American Museum of Natural History.

houses of ill repute, critics suggested it made more sense to regulate them—a debate rekindled in 1984 when a committee from the City Club of Portland recommended legalizing prostitution.

Lane had a fine touch for the dramatic. One day, after inspecting curbing installed in the Irvington neighborhood, he personally took a pick and sledgehammer to the shoddy segments.

U'Ren remained a powerful figure at the state level into the early 1910s. Voters quickly approved measures he backed to spur direct primaries, tougher anti-corruption laws, and the right to recall elected officials. But eventually his failures began to outnumber his successes. Voters repeatedly rejected the one societal reform he really wanted: a radical tax on land devised by social philosopher Henry George, who thought his "single tax" would spur

JOHN H. MITCHELL
For years the most powerful political figure in the state, Mitchell served 22 years in the U.S. Senate. It was sometimes said Oregon was run from his Portland law offices, where his clients included the railroad companies.

labor and productivity while breaking the power of the idle rich. U'Ren also got nowhere when he tried to run for governor and the U.S. Senate. Some of his ideas couldn't even attract enough signatures to make the ballot.

In the last years of his life, he lived quietly with his wife in a downtown Portland apartment. In an interview a few months before his death at age 90 in 1949, he remained fiercely proud of the initiative system and opposed any attempts to weaken it. Occasionally visitors from as far away as Europe would stop by to meet the man who once so personified citizen activism. But not many remembered.

In 1946, Oregon writer Stewart Holbrook tried to explain U'Ren's influence for a new generation. Accurately enough, it was in a book titled *Lost Men of American History*.

Highway engineer Samuel Lancaster leads a party along the Columbia River Highway at Shepperd's Dell on the opening day of the road in 1915.

New Ideas in the 1910s

MODERN OREGON BEGINS TO TAKE SHAPE
AS CARS BECOME ALL THE RAGE,
WOMEN GAIN VOTING RIGHTS,
AND A VISIONARY GOVERNOR PRESERVES
THE STATE'S BEACHES FOR THE PUBLIC

By Jeff Mapes

Abigail Scott Duniway, severely weakened by illness at the age of 78, took days to pen the proclamation in her own hand. She could write but only a few words at a time before giving in to exhaustion.

Finally, on November 30, 1912, Duniway presented the finished document to the youthful, charismatic governor of Oregon, Oswald West. With the scrawl of his signature, women in Oregon at last could vote.

When one looks back today at an old photograph of that emotional ceremony, which certified the victory of a ballot measure on women's suffrage, Governor West, with his high collar, and Abigail Duniway, with her quaint head covering, appear to be relics from Oregon's pioneer past. On the contrary, at that historic moment, West and Duniway helped to usher in the modern Oregon.

It's not just that Oswald West first preserved Oregon's beaches for the public and that Duniway dominated the women's suffrage movement in the Northwest. Instead, it is that both helped establish so many of the qualities we've come to hold special about Oregon, from our deep-seated egalitarianism to our urge to protect the scenic wonders that serve as a daily reminder that we don't live in Kansas.

In the second decade of the century, Oregon was in the middle of a remarkable social and political transformation that would last until World War I. As governor during one of the most productive four-year terms in state history, West presided over a dizzying number of reforms that established government as a force to protect the average man . . . and woman. A state commission set minimum wages and working conditions for women and children. A new Public Utility Commission regulated monopoly services. The creation of a workers' compensation system finally ensured that people injured on the job would not simply be discarded. Other new laws cracked down on shady stock deals and other corporate swindles. West pursued prison reform, a system of juvenile courts, and the creation of a state fish and game commission. Amid all of this, in 1913 he persuaded the Legislature to declare the state's beaches a public highway, forever owned by the citizens. At the time, it went almost unnoticed.

Above: *Governor Oswald West protected the public's access to beaches in 1913 by declaring them public highways, drawing such travelers as these* (right) *in a 1914 Overland auto at Hug Point, south of Cannon Beach. Far right: Work crews, posing during construction of the Columbia River Highway in 1915, gave Oregonians a chance to travel amid the state's beauty in comfort.*

ecales Cannon Beach Or.

Working on Columbia Highway 1915

NEW CARS, NEW ROADS

Of course, coastal development would not become a huge issue until the automobile and the road network reached all corners of the state. But that, too, started in the 1910s. At the beginning of the decade, Oregon had fewer than 2,500 registered cars. By 1920, there were more than 103,000—about one for every eight people. The newspapers were full of car ads that hyped the new technological wonders. (A 1913 Buick, 25-horsepower, two-person roadster went for $1,060. But if you wanted 40 horses, room for five passengers, and electric lighting, that would set you back $1,800.)

The entire nation was falling in love with the automobile, and Oregon was no exception. The ubiquitous mud of Western Oregon, however, severely limited automobile travel. If you lived in Portland, you didn't go fly-fishing on the Deschutes for the weekend. Modern travel, unless it was by rail, required paved roads. One of the earliest grand examples of the possibilities of automotive travel came with the creation of the Columbia River Highway.

Built between 1913 and 1915, the Columbia River Highway did more than move goods and people. Sam Hill, a railroad attorney and entrepreneur with the promotional enthusiasm of a circus barker, envisioned the highway as a way to bring people close to the waterfalls and other wonders of the gorge. He thought it would not only attract more tourists, which would stimulate more rail traffic to Oregon, but also induce more people to settle and invest in the region. The highway, built with the goal of being its own work of art, also changed people's relationship with nature. They could travel easily amid its spectacular mountainscapes and appreciate its beauty without surrendering modern comforts.

Oregon further cemented the age of good roads in 1919 by passing the nation's first gasoline tax to pay for them. In typical Oregon fashion, though, a tight-fisted reason was behind it. Property taxpayers complained they didn't want to foot the cost of roads for joy-riding rich people.

Above: *Suffragist Abigail Scott Duniway was an indefatigable writer and lecturer who mentored a generation of Northwest women.*
Above right: *After years of effort, she signs the proclamation certifying that women have the right to vote in Oregon as Governor Oswald West and Viola M. Coe, acting president of the Oregon State Equal Suffrage League, look on.*
Right: *She later casts a ballot in Portland in 1914.*

LONG FIGHT FOR SUFFRAGE

Despite chronic health problems following six difficult childbirths, Abigail Scott Duniway began her public campaign for women's suffrage in 1870 at age 36 and kept at it for more than four decades. She incessantly traveled the Northwest, bringing her message to women—and men—in the most isolated of communities. For 16 years, she edited a weekly newspaper, the *New Northwest,* which contained everything from her serialized novels to an appreciation of the harshness of frontier life for women. Duniway had known something about hardship herself. Born in Illinois in 1834, she came to Oregon by covered wagon. Her mother and a younger brother fell ill and died during the trip.

She mentored a generation of suffragists in Oregon and Washington and—long before the rise of feminism—spoke movingly of the value of women's lives and the work they did. She wrote of the frustration she felt as a young wife on a Molalla River ranch when her husband's friends dropped in, expecting a free meal or even a quick laundry for their dirty clothes.

"The most lingering of my many regrets," she wrote, "is the fact that I was often compelled to neglect my little children, while spending my time in the kitchen, or at the churn or wash tub, doing heavy work for hale and hearty men."

Hot-tempered and blunt, Duniway "unfortunately had the kind of personality that riled people up," explained her biographer, Ruth Barnes Moynihan. Her personality exacerbated the long-running dispute Duniway had with many suffragists regarding the issue of prohibition. Many activists seeking the women's vote saw it as a means to outlaw alcohol, which they believed to be the chief evil that led men to abuse women and neglect their families. Duniway thought the biggest problem was a lack of equality for women, one not solved by prohibition. Beyond that, she feared men in Oregon would be extremely reluctant to give women the right to vote if they thought it would lead to a ban on alcohol.

Of course, part of the blame lay with Duniway's own brother, Harvey Scott, the influential editor of *The Oregonian* from 1865 until his death in 1910. Brilliant, tough, and ever scheming, Scott played equal parts journalist, businessman, and politician as he built the newspaper into one of the state's

A. E. DOYLE
The architect opened his own practice in 1907, lavishing personal attention on houses for Portland's leading families. He would design many of Portland's major buildings, including several banks, the Public Service Building, the Central Library, the Meier & Frank Store, Reed College, and the Benson Hotel.

SIMON BENSON
Oregon's most prominent timber baron, Benson sold his empire for $4.5 million in 1910 but continued to play a significant role in the state's development. In addition to building the Benson Hotel, he donated Multnomah Falls to public use and played a key role in development of the Columbia River Highway.

most powerful institutions. The relationship between the two siblings was Shakespearean in its complexity (and, suitably, the subject of at least one stage play). Duniway resented that, because of her gender, she could never hope to achieve her brother's lofty position. But that didn't stop her from accepting tokens of his wealth and influence. Scott also would hold out the promise of supporting his sister's causes, only to throw the weight of *The Oregonian* against women's suffrage whenever it came up for a vote.

Women's suffrage was defeated five times at the polls before being approved in 1912. No state voted more times on the issue than Oregon.

THE RISE OF A REFORMER

Oswald West was heavily influenced by Duniway. He first heard her speak when he was a ten-year-old growing up in Salem. She challenged the crowd gathered in a town square, saying, "Don't you consider your mother as good, if not better, than an ordinary Salem saloon bum?"

West whispered to himself, "Sure I do." In fact, he adored his mother and disdained his father, an alcoholic who could have fit Duniway's derisive description. West became both an ardent suffragist and a prohibitionist.

If Duniway was an archetype showing the power of individual activism in Oregon, West blazed a path showing how a politician without wealth or influence could win high office. A protégé of Governor George Chamberlain, a reform-minded Democrat who served from 1903 to 1909, West had little name recognition or campaign money when he sought the governorship in 1910. But he ran a masterful grassroots campaign that championed the initiative system and the other political reforms of William Simon U'Ren. Most importantly, he successfully labeled his Republican opponent a pawn of the political bosses. West won despite the Republicans' 3-to-1 voter registration advantage.

In office, West was colorful, engaging, and smart in persuading the Republican-led Legislature to go along with reforms that headed off more radical change. The nation was at a high-water mark of the Progressive Era. A new class of well-educated, middle-class urbanites no longer accepted the domination of the old political machines.

Depending on what account of the times you

"Dedication ceremonies "Vista House"" Columbia River Highway Ore. May 5th 1918 Cross & D

Above: *Oregonians flock to the new Crown Point Vista House, dedicated on May 15, 1918, in the Columbia Gorge.* Right: *The flight of Silas Christofferson off the roof of the Multnomah Hotel in 1912 was part of a stunt to publicize the Rose Festival. About 50,000 watched as he began a flight that ended successfully 12 minutes later in Vancouver, Washington.*

Champion buckaroo Tillie Baldwin draws cheers at the 1912 Pendleton Round-Up.

read, Portland was either a font of radicalism or a sleepy, bourgeois city. Portlander John Reed, a famous left-wing journalist later interred in the wall of the Kremlin, returned home after covering Pancho Villa's exploits in Mexico and declared his hometown "as dull as ever." But it also proved to be fertile ground for C. E. S. Wood, a swashbuckling poet, lawyer, painter, and former soldier. He bounced between the Arlington Club and anarchist meetings with ease. He earned a then-amazing $1 million commission for brokering a huge public land transfer into private hands—and defended birth control pioneer Margaret Sanger on obscenity charges after she was arrested in Portland for selling the booklet *Family Planning*.

As West rode the wave of reform, he could be convinced of his own rightness, no matter where it led him. In the same 1912 election that gave women the right to vote, Oregonians (or at least the men who could vote in that election) refused to heed West's pleas to abolish the death penalty. West, who

HARRY LANE
A reformist mayor of Portland, Lane became a U.S. senator and cast one of the six votes against U.S. entry into World War I. He came under a firestorm of criticism in Oregon and died of a stroke seven weeks later.

had suspended the sentences of everyone on Death Row until after the election, promptly announced he would once again proceed with capital punishment. He told the superintendent of the Oregon State Penitentiary to hang four convicted murderers on December 13.

The day before the scheduled executions, a delegation from Portland traveled to Salem to urge West to reconsider. One member of the delegation, Frances C. R. Grothjean, a Portland artist, flung herself at West's knees and prayed for him to spare the men's lives. Wait, the group pleaded, until the next election, when women also can vote.

West was unmoved. "I intend to do tomorrow what I believe will bring about abolition of capital punishment most speedily," he told the group. "If these men do not go to the gallows tomorrow, capital punishment will not be abolished in this state during our lives."

The four men were hanged, two at a time, the next day. Two years later, voters abolished the death

PEOPLE

Population reaches 672,765 in 1910; men outnumber women 384,265 to 288,500.

103,001 are "foreign-born"; Native American population drops by nearly one-eighth, to 3,477, since 1900.

Salem overtakes Astoria as the second-largest city, with 14,094.

GETTING AROUND

Oregon begins issuing license plates in 1911— black numbers on a yellow background.

The state highway system comprises 2,900 miles of roads in 1914.

Portland streetcar system's 526 cars carry 258,717 riders a day in 1912.

Oregon's first public airfield opens in Eastmoreland in 1914; the first commercial airline service is provided by Oregon, Washington & Idaho Airplane Company in 1919.

Autos rev up

The automobile took off in Oregon, and Ford even opened an assembly plant in Portland in 1914.

Thousands of registered autos

120 — 103,790

80 —

40 — 2,493

0 — 1910 1920

Source: Oregon Blue Book

HOME

A five-room bungalow on a 40-by-100-foot lot near Rose City Park advertises for $3,300; furnished rooms available for $1 to $3 a week; Christmas trees delivered to homes for 49 cents; fresh salmon sells for 15 cents a pound.

WORK

A chemist is sought for $5.52 a day, and an experienced waitress for 25 cents an hour for two hours a day.

POLITICS

More than half (173,983) of Oregon's 304,730 registered voters in 1914 are Republican; 78,891 are Democrats; 16,432 are members of the Prohibition Party.

PLAY

A nationally successful documentary on the Pendleton Round-Up, *Where Cowboy Is King,* is filmed in 1914.

The Majestic Theater opens as a vaudeville house in downtown Portland in 1913.

A. C. Gilbert of Salem invents the Erector Set in 1913; he is the first toy manufacturer to advertise in national magazines and sells 30 million sets.

ENVIRONMENT

The declining elk population prompts the creation of a refuge in Wallowa County.

SCHOOL

Oregon's 118,412 public school students—80.2 percent of Oregonians ages 5 to 17—attend an average of 121.8 days a year in 1910.

NATIONAL FIRSTS

Sister Miriam Theresa and Father Edwin O'Hara push through the nation's first effective minimum wage law for women in 1913.

Portland's National Guard unit becomes the first in the nation to mobilize for World War I.

WAR

44,166 Oregonians serve in World War I; 1,030 are killed and 1,100 wounded.

MEDICAL BREAKTHROUGHS

In 1910, Dr. W. H. Lytle, the Oregon state veterinarian, discovers "eggs laid by tubercular hens serve as a medium to spread tuberculosis"; he also discovers that the virus is killed if the eggs are well cooked.

CRIME AND JUSTICE

Chief of police reports Portland is free of crime in April; but there were 620 arrests for drunkenness, and police were keeping "women of the town" on the move.

Margaret Sanger, founder of America's birth control movement, is arrested in Portland in 1916 for distributing obscene material: a pamphlet explaining birth control.

Celebrators prepare to dedicate the Interstate Bridge on February 14, 1917.

penalty. (It was later restored, abolished again, and restored once again.)

West pursued fighting vice and drink with equal zeal. He tried to combat prostitution, seizing on a Portland vice commission study that found 21 percent of the reported disease in Portland was venereal in nature. But he had more success going after booze. Attitudes about alcohol had been changing, and many came to see prohibition, or at least the closing of saloons, as a way to control the increasing number of immigrants they saw as inferior.

Today, we associate Henry Weinhard with the warm and funny depictions of frontier life portrayed in his company's beer ads. But West regarded him in terms that would now be reserved for a crack cocaine dealer.

"Weinhard's brewery won't rule the state of Oregon," West declared. "There isn't a brick in the brewery that doesn't represent a broken heart."

By 1914, voters were ready to go along. Thanks in large part to the women's vote, Oregonians voted to close the saloons and shut down the breweries and distillers. If you wanted to drink in Oregon—

SAM HILL
A Seattle railroad lawyer and entrepreneur, Sam Hill was the spark plug behind the Columbia River Highway, one of the finest early examples of the road builder's art.

legally, that is—you had to do so in the privacy of your own home, with beverages imported from out of state. In 1916, voters approved "bone-dry" prohibition—three years before it was adopted nationally.

A FEAR OF DIFFERENCES

Progressivism in Oregon had its limits. In 1916, voters narrowly refused to repeal unenforceable sections of the state Constitution that forbade African-Americans from voting. The burgeoning sense of equality had not yet extended to people of color. In fact, white Oregonians were all too ready to fear anybody who was different. The opening of the Panama Canal in 1915 provided new trade opportunities for the Northwest, but it also incited new fears about immigration. The spreading war in Europe also incited a nativism and reactionism that began to sweep Oregon and the nation. By the time the United States entered World War I in 1917, war fervor was at its height. Portland's National Guard unit was the first in the country to mobilize, and the town fathers rushed to change street names of Germanic origin.

1910

Women's suffrage and prohibition fail at the polls. Meier & Frank Company begins using trucks instead of horse-drawn wagons for deliveries. The Oregon State Tuberculosis Hospital opens. Reed College is founded. Jantzen begins making fabric. The Farmers Union holds its first state convention in The Dalles. Fire destroys the business district in Bonanza.

1911

The Legislature authorizes automobile license plates. The Oregon Public Utility Commission forms.

1912

Oregon, which has voted on suffrage more times than any other state, grants women the right to vote. The Pendleton Round-Up stages its first competition. Portland's first gas station opens. The Benson Hotel begins serving. The Steel Bridge opens. The Royal Rosarians organize. Portland hosts the first professional hockey game in the nation.

1913

Governor Oswald West signs a law making beaches public highways. New laws provide for workers' compensation, regulation of securities offerings, and employment protections for women and children. Willamette University Department of Medicine merges with University of Oregon Medical School in Portland. Hillcrest School for Girls opens near Salem. Portland's Central Library and the Multnomah County Courthouse are built. The Legislature requires counties to levy tax to aid mothers with dependent children. The State Highway Commission forms. Portland voters replace the 15-member, part-time City Council with four full-time commissioners and a mayor. Mount Tabor identified as an extinct volcano. The Broadway Bridge opens.

1914

Oregon voters adopt public prohibition and approve initiative to abolish the death penalty. Governor West declares martial law in Copperfield, a rowdy Baker County mining town, and sends his secretary, Fern Hobbs, to restore order. A Ford assembly plant opens at Southeast 12th and Division. Molalla Buckaroo begins as celebration to welcome the Willamette Valley Southern Railway. Fire sweeps the Bandon business district. The NAACP organizes a Portland chapter.

1915

The first caravan of cars leaves Portland for Hood River over the new Columbia River Highway. St. Johns and Linnton vote to join Portland.

1916

Two units of the state's National Guard are called for service against Pancho Villa in the Mexican Border War. Portland's Public Safety Commission begins keeping records of traffic accidents. The U.S. National Bank building opens. Oregonians narrowly refuse to repeal a state constitutional amendment that bars African-Americans from voting—even though such a ban was long overruled by the nation's 14th Amendment.

1917

2,000 members of the Third Infantry Regiment march off to World War I. The University of Oregon drubs Pennsylvania 14-0 in the Rose Bowl. The Interstate Bridge spans the Columbia River.

1918

The State Board of Health records 3,675 deaths from an influenza epidemic. Portland voters reject home for dependents and delinquent children. Crown Point Vista House opens.

1919

The Legislature approves a gasoline tax for highway construction, the first in the nation.

Oregon troops on their way to World War I in 1917 march under a liberty arch at Southwest Sixth Avenue and Morrison Street. More than 44,000 Oregonians served in the war.

Oregon Senator Harry Lane, one of only six senators to vote against going to war, was so pilloried by the local establishment that he died of a stroke seven weeks later. J. Henry Albers, the German-born president of the milling company whose silos can still be seen at the west end of the Broadway Bridge in Portland, was arrested and charged with sedition after he drank too much on a train from San Francisco and began singing in German.

In addition to the stress of the war, an influenza outbreak in 1918 killed 3,675 in Oregon as it swept across the country.

After the November 11 armistice that year, a postwar wave of strikes further exacerbated tensions. The Industrial Workers of the World, known as the Wobblies, were stronger in Washington than in Oregon. But the labor activists were widely derided here as dangerous radicals.

It was a time of the Red Scare, not of reform. The progressive era had run its course. Duniway died in 1915 at age 80, five years before women's suffrage was made part of the U.S. Constitution.

JOHN REED
A native of Portland, Reed was eventually buried in the wall of the Kremlin. He was a globetrotting journalist who fell in love with and eventually married Louise Bryant, the wife of a Portland dentist. Reed wrote *Ten Days That Shook the World* before returning to Russia in 1919. He befriended Vladimir Lenin and was barred from returning to the U.S.

As for West, he served just one term and declined to run for re-election. He said he had accomplished most of what he set out to do, and now he needed to secure his financial future. He eventually became a lobbyist for Pacific Power & Light Company and was a frequent letter writer to newspapers. He died in 1960 at age 87.

West's daughter, Portland resident Jean McHugh, remembers her father's pride in having taken the first steps toward preserving public ownership of the beaches. He did it with the clever strategy of telling the Legislature it was making a huge addition to the state highway system at no cost. In truth, West, who had built a cabin overlooking Haystack Rock at Cannon Beach, viewed the beauty of the coast in almost sacred terms. He wasn't thinking of transportation. So it was not surprising that, one day in the late 1940s, McHugh remembers her father disgustedly looking at the cars cramming the beach.

"This isn't what I did that for," he said, shaking his head. It would be left to a future generation to complete his vision.

A Portland police "shotgun squad" guards a bank messenger with a satchel of money in 1927.

ROARING WITH THE 1920s

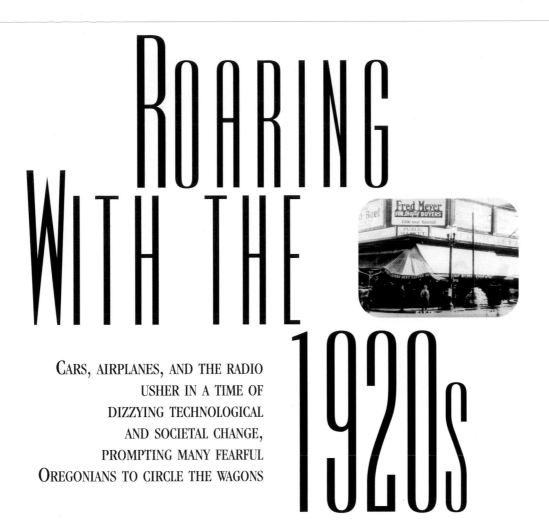

CARS, AIRPLANES, AND THE RADIO
USHER IN A TIME OF
DIZZYING TECHNOLOGICAL
AND SOCIETAL CHANGE,
PROMPTING MANY FEARFUL
OREGONIANS TO CIRCLE THE WAGONS

By Sura Rubenstein

As fiery crosses lit up the night sky on Eugene's Skinner Butte, on Portland's Mount Tabor, and in towns and cities from the Oregon coast to the Idaho border, thousands of men swore secret oaths and hid their faces under white hoods. Still, their unexpected strength jolted the state. Even Governor Ben Olcott was taken by surprise.

"We woke up one morning and found that the Klan had about gained control of the state," he told his colleagues at the 1922 National Governors' Conference. "Practically not a word has been raised against them."

Although Oregon was not the only part of the country contributing to the resurgence of the 19th-century racist group, it was among the strongest Ku Klux Klan states west of the Rockies.

The first Klan organizers came to Southern Oregon in 1921, and before long the KKK was holding outdoor initiations on Portland's Mount Scott as part of the city's Rose Festival. In less than two years, the Klan recruited 14,000 members in Oregon, giving it perhaps the highest per-capita membership in the country. And in the 1922 election, it succeeded in unseating Congressman Clifton McArthur and Governor Olcott, and electing two Multnomah County commissioners and a slate of state legislators. It also helped pass a nationally notorious initiative aimed at putting Catholic schools out of business.

Although the Klan's influence waned by mid-decade, its rapid growth and political impact in Oregon illuminated both longstanding prejudices and popular reaction against the moral and economic frenzy that was Jazz Age America. Throughout the 1920s, a stunning array of technological advances, from the radio to air travel, transformed everyday life and linked the end of the Oregon Trail to national trends and fears as never before. As Oregonians recovered from the country's first lengthy international war and coped with staggering changes, many grasped for the past.

"The Klan's members saw themselves as a force for moral improvement," said Portland historian David A. Horowitz, editor of *Inside the Klavern*, an annotated collection of the records of the 1920s La Grande Klan.

At a time when writers such as Sinclair Lewis pilloried small-town life in popular books such as *Babbitt,* the Klan embraced social "purity" movements such as Prohibition and "100 percent Americanism." The Klan found fertile ground in Oregon, a state that was more than 80 percent white and U.S.-born and 90 percent Protestant. Oregon's 1859 Constitution barred African-Americans from the state, and even though the 14th Amendment to the U.S. Constitution made that provision moot in 1868, Oregonians didn't repeal it until 1926.

Anti-Japanese sentiments also were part of the state's social fabric, as was an anti-Catholicism that historians date to the early days of white settlement.

Horowitz emphasizes that the Klan of the 1920s was a mainstream movement that included police chiefs, elected officials, and businessmen. It offered a comforting group identity, rather like the Masons or the Rotary, he says, and a way to respond to confusing social change.

Top: *W.K. Newell, federal prohibition director for Oregon, and Sheriff Frank Richard join Albany Women's Christian Temperance Union members to display illegal liquor and equipment seized in Albany on November 21, 1926.*
Bottom: *Portland celebrates Broadway Theater Day on August 25, 1926, along Broadway. For the first time in the 1920s, more people went to the movies on a Sunday than went to church.*

OREGON CONNECTS WITH THE NATION

The Roaring Twenties were a time of dizzying transitions. Suspended between World War I and the Great Depression, the decade was an awkward bridge between traditional culture and the modern world. F. Scott Fitzgerald, whose first novel became a best-seller in 1920, described a cynical post–World War I generation that found "all Gods dead, all wars fought, all faiths in man shaken."

At the same time, an evangelical revival and fundamentalist crusade pitted Darwinian evolution against creationism in the 1925 Scopes "Monkey Trial." The fundamentalists prevailed in court but were derided in the new mass media. There was a popular romance with science, and even Albert Einstein's theory of relativity became a common topic of public debate.

The first commercial radio stations connected Oregon with the nation in a way never before possible. Advertising and Hollywood films celebrated a new consumer culture and, for the first time, more people went to the movies on a Sunday than went to church. Women's suffrage and Prohibition, adopted in Oregon in the 1910s, spread across the country. Dance halls such as Cotillion Hall and McElroy's Spanish Ballroom drew young people returning from

the war or those who just wanted to spread their wings in an era of "flaming youth" that promised new freedoms. The flapper, often shown with a cigarette in her mouth, typified the modern woman. The divorce rate shot up, in Oregon and across the country.

In 1923, the editor of La Grande's *Evening Observer* pointed out that only Nevada outpaced Oregon's divorce rate. The paper declared divorce a "menace to America" and noted that Americans were ending marriages at the rate of one every four minutes.

It was a time of new mobility, both on land and in the air. Cars gave ordinary people a new sense of freedom. By 1920, there was an auto for every eight Oregonians. In the late 1920s, notes urban historian Carl Abbott, Portlanders spent as much on their autos as they did on food: $42 million a year. Portland entered the era of commercial air travel in 1926 but had to use Pearson Field in Vancouver, Washington, as its airport. In 1927, the city of Portland brought in celebrity aviator Charles A. Lindbergh to dedicate its own airport on Swan Island—just four months after he'd made the first solo trans-Atlantic flight in the *Spirit of St. Louis*.

Nationwide, the city was in ascendancy, and rural life seemed left in its wake. By 1930, for the first time, more than half of Oregon's residents lived in urban areas.

GEORGE BAKER
The gregarious Baker, who owned a popular theater company, was elected Portland mayor in 1917 with a promise that "smoke-stacks will be as numerous as trees." He served for 16 years with the support of businesses, cracking down on labor organizers and suspected communists.

Across the country, a postwar plunge in farm prices created new crises. In Oregon, farmers' purchasing power dropped by nearly 40 percent between 1919 and 1921. Oregon's powerful U.S. Senator Charles McNary led a campaign for federal farm aid that would last for more than a decade and signal a profound shift in the role of government.

"The premise was that government had a responsibility to promote economic and social justice in hard times," wrote his biographer, Steve Neal, in *McNary of Oregon*.

REDEFINING AMERICANISM

After World War I, even as President Woodrow Wilson unsuccessfully pushed for the country to join the new League of Nations, Americans yearned to return to an imagined prewar Eden.

"One Hundred Percent Americanism, with its built-in implication that that which was alien was evil, was locked in as part of the national ethic," wrote Malcolm Clark Jr. in a 1974 article in the *Oregon Historical Quarterly*. "Reasonable men were perfectly aware it was not possible to turn back into the past. But even reasonable men were resentful that it was not."

Left: *The Battleship USS* Oregon *arrives on June 14, 1925, at the Portland harbor, where it would be moored until 1942, drawing 2,000 visitors a month. The ship was launched in 1893 and played a vital role in the Spanish-American War.* Above: *Portland auto dealers line up their cars on Terwilliger Boulevard. By 1929, more cars and trucks were registered in Multnomah County—90,000 plus—than had been found in the entire state at the beginning of the decade.*

Catholics, Jews, and immigrants bore the brunt of America's cultural discontent. The aftershocks of the 1917 Russian Revolution fueled a homegrown Red Scare, aggravated by the 1919 Seattle General Strike and local labor disputes. President Warren G. Harding, speaking in Portland on July 4, 1923, just a month before his unexpected death, echoed a popular theme when he emphasized the importance of limiting immigration to those "mentally and morally qualified" to become "true" American citizens.

Fears of papal influence scuttled the 1924 and 1928 presidential bids of New York Governor Al Smith, the first Catholic to run for the nation's highest office. Oregon's *Klamath Falls Herald* in 1923 actually reported that Catholics celebrated the birth of boys by burying guns and ammunition underneath churches "in preparation for the day when the government is to be overthrown on behalf of the pope."

The Japanese, who had begun arriving in the state in significant numbers only within the preceding generation, quickly became another target. Oregon's Japanese population had grown from just two in 1880 to 2,501 in 1900, as young men were imported for what was expected to be temporary work on the railroads, in the forests, and in the canneries. By 1920, as "picture brides" from Japan joined the men

RUTH BARNETT
During a span of 50 years, Barnett performed an estimated 40,000 abortions, entering the abortion business in 1918. By the 1930s, Barnett was working openly in the Broadway Building (where Nordstrom now stands) in downtown Portland. After being in and out of jail in the 1950s, she was sent to prison for five months for manslaughter by abortion in 1968.

for whom the United States became a permanent home, the state's Japanese-American population shot up to 4,151. The largest communities were in Hood River, Astoria, and the Portland area. In east Multnomah County and Hood River, Japanese farmers soon dominated some truck farming crops. In 1919, a group of Hood River residents, which included prominent white citizens, formed an "Anti-Asiatic Association" and took an oath asserting that the valley was threatened by a Japanese takeover. Even Olcott—who later became the first U.S. governor to publicly denounce the Klan—in 1921 urged the Legislature to take action "to preserve our lands and our resources for the people of our own race and nationality."

In 1920, Oregon's Japanese-Americans owned a fraction of just 1 percent of the state's total acreage. But by 1923, the Klan-dominated Legislature pushed through an Alien Land Law similar to those in California and Washington barring Japanese land ownership. The legislation completed a bulwark of legal discrimination along the West Coast that stood until 1947. At times, anti-Japanese prejudice erupted into violence. On July 12, 1925, a mob of about 300 in the coastal town of Toledo routed 35 Japanese who had just arrived to work in the Pacific Spruce mill.

Minoru Yasui, whose family settled in Hood River and who in 1939 became Oregon's first Japanese-American attorney, said the immigrants weren't prepared for the violence. "Much of it sprang from race hatred, stubborn, bitter, and unreasoning," he wrote in a 1940 article in *The Sunday Oregonian*. "And some of it, of course, was prompted by the fact that the early Japanese worked for less, lived on less, and frequently prospered more."

REBIRTH OF THE KLAN

Ironically, the Klan was both a reaction to and a product of the new mass culture of the 1920s. Its resurgence was sparked by D. W. Griffith's 1915 *The Birth of a Nation*, which romanticized Klansmen as defenders of traditional values.

Launched with a cross burning atop Georgia's Stone Mountain in 1915, the resurgent Klan didn't catch fire until founder William Joseph Simmons hired two publicists to promote it and until organizers got cash incentives to recruit. But it soon became a mass movement, drawing as many as 5 million members, and even President Harding was rumored to be a Klansman.

In Portland, Fred L. Gifford, a Minnesota native, quit his $250-a-month job as a manager for the Northwestern Electrical Company to take a $600-a-month job as Exalted Cyclops of the local Klan. He soon became Grand Dragon of Oregon, then Deputy Wizard for all states west of the Rockies. In general, the group wasn't violent. But when it began organizing in the Medford area in 1921, Klansmen held "necktie parties," or near-lynchings, of two African-Americans suspected of bootlegging and of a piano dealer who'd filed a lawsuit against a Klan member.

Olcott, when he learned of the Klan's necktie parties, denounced the Klan just days before the 1922 May primary. And he soon became one of its first political victims.

"Oregon needs no masked night riders, no invisible empire, to control her affairs," he said in a statement decrying the violence that had occurred in Medford. "The true spirit of Americanism resents bigotry, abhors secret machinations and

Above: *Fred Meyer opened his first store in 1922 at Southwest Fifth Avenue and Yamhill in Portland.*
Right: *A crowd gathers to listen to an early radio broadcast from KGW in Portland.*

Left: *Ku Klux Klan members march on East Main Street in Ashland in the 1920s. In less than two years, the Klan recruited 14,000 members in Oregon.*

terrorism, and demands that those who speak for and in her cause speak openly, with their faces to the sun."

Olcott's statements enraged the Klan, which already was supporting Olcott's GOP challenger, Charles Hall. "I have only to say that the Ku Klux Klan is a law-abiding organization," Gifford shot back, "based on the maintenance of white supremacy and the Christian religion."

After Olcott squeaked by Hall, Gifford threw Klan support behind Democrat Walter Pierce, a La Grande rancher who unseated Olcott in November. In that election, voters also supported a Klan-endorsed initiative that effectively outlawed private and parochial schools. The "compulsory school law" was drafted by the Masons and supported by a coalition of nativist groups and Governor-elect Pierce. Under the banner of "One Flag, One School, One Language," it required students between the ages of 8 and 16 to attend public schools—with the aim of "Americanizing" them. The law, however, never took effect and quickly was declared

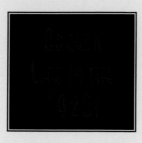

PEOPLE

Population reaches 783,389 in 1920; split in half between rural and urban residents; "Indians," "Chinese," and "Japanese" are counted within one group and total 12,099; 2,144 are "Negroes."

Portland moves up to 24th-largest city in nation.

HOME

Most popular baby names in 1920: Mary, Dorothy, Helen, John, William, and James.

Average family size: 3.86.

Stark-Davis Company in Portland advertises a kitchen sink for $22 and a bathtub for $33.

At Olds, Wortman & King, dolls cost between $1.25 and $11.

Technology comes home

Rapid technological changes were reflected in daily life, such as the growth of the telephone.

Assessed value of phone companies in Oregon

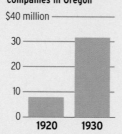

Source: Oregon Blue Book

WORK

In 1920, 78 percent of males and 18 percent of females over age 10 are working.

Oregon's per capita income is $668; U.S. average is $699.

In 1929, auto sales are up 22 percent, agricultural product sales increase by $5 million, and manufacturing increases by 31 percent.

PLAY

Round-trip train fare from Portland to the coast in 1920 is $4.50.

In December 1920, Julius Sax, owner of the New Grand and Princess theaters in Portland, predicts demise of small theaters because of costs of making motion pictures.

Buster Keaton films *The General* in Cottage Grove in 1926.

BREAKTHROUGHS

In 1920, Civil War veteran Samuel Gray receives a patent on his washing machine that can "perfectly clean 50 pieces in 11 minutes"—he anticipates selling each machine for $11 to $15.

First radio license is issued in Oregon in 1922.

GETTING AROUND

Oregon enacts its first driving laws in 1920; driver must be 16, have five days' driving experience, and pay 25 cents.

Maximum driving speed increases to 25 miles per hour.

By 1927, Oregon registers 220,000 automobiles, up from 104,000 in 1920.

Oregon's first air passenger service begins in 1928: flights to Portland, Seattle, Medford, San Francisco, and Los Angeles.

ENVIRONMENT

First land donated to Oregon specifically for a park in 1922 for the Sarah Helmick State Park in Polk County.

The winter of 1928-29 has measurable snow for 21 straight days in Portland.

SCHOOL

In 1920, 151,028, or 84.1 percent of children between 5 and 17, attend Oregon's public schools an average of 137.5 days a year; 6,051 students attend private and parochial schools

The 7,778 public school teachers earn an average of $870 a year.

POLITICS

Republican Calvin Coolidge wins Oregon in 1924; Independent Robert M. LaFollette receives nearly 900 more votes than the third-place Democrat, John W. Davis.

CRIME AND JUSTICE

By 1928, 629 people are imprisoned, compared with 9,246 today.

Crowds gather for the dedication of the Astoria column, honoring Captain Robert Gray, Lewis and Clark, and John Jacob Astor, July 22, 1926.

unconstitutional by U.S. District Court and in 1925 by the U.S. Supreme Court.

Even before the Supreme Court ruling, however, the Oregon Klan began losing steam. Internal feuding, charges of corruption against Fred Gifford, and the indictment and recall of the Klan's Multnomah County commissioners for graft involving bridge contracts all took a toll. McNary spurned Gifford's offer to switch his endorsement from Portland Mayor George Baker in the 1924 GOP Senate race, and in the primary McNary beat the popular Portland mayor by a 2-to-1 ratio in Portland alone.

By the decade's end, Oregon's Klan membership had dwindled to just a few dozen. It had lost one of its main issues when immigration restrictions became national policy by 1924, and the courts

BEATRICE CANNADY Cannady graduated from Lewis and Clark law school in 1922 and was editor of the *Advocate* newspaper. She campaigned for extending public education to African-Americans in the Northwest.

killed its plans for compulsory public education. Ultimately, however, historian Horowitz thinks the Klan failed because it was too divisive. Instead of the social cohesion it sought, the Klan brought disruption.

In La Grande, for example, a town with a sizable Catholic population, the Klan urged its members to patronize only businesses owned "100 percent" by white Protestants. Key targets of this campaign were a German-American luncheonette and La Grande's largest bank, whose chief financial officer was Catholic. But the Klan couldn't even persuade many of its own members to stay away from the luncheonette. And a Klansman who sat on the board of a rival bank urged others to hold off on the bank boycott. "The boycotts just didn't serve the needs of the business interests," Horowitz says.

1920

Voters reverse their 1914 decision and reinstate the death penalty. Harvard defeats Oregon 7-6 in the Rose Bowl. Community Chest organizes to support social welfare.

1921

The Port of Portland acquires Swan Island land for an airport. The Ku Klux Klan organizes in Oregon and stages three "necktie parties," or near-lynchings, near Medford. J. K. Gill moves to a new ten-story building.

1922

Vice President Calvin Coolidge dedicates the Rough Rider statue of Theodore Roosevelt in the South Park Blocks. Fire destroys Astoria's business district and leaves 2,000 homeless. Fred Meyer opens his first grocery store. Steinfeld's Products Company starts pickling. Portland's first commercial radio station, KGW, goes on air.

1923

Democrat Walter Pierce wins the governorship with support of the Ku Klux Klan. The Legislature passes a law, primarily aimed at the Japanese, banning aliens from owning land. State begins licensing trucks. DeAutremont brothers commit the nation's "last great train robbery" south of Ashland. A fire in Arlington destroys the Grand Hotel, city hall, the fire station, and several businesses.

1924

President Coolidge is heard on KGW via the first nationwide radio hookup. The Portland Junior Symphony forms. Thomas Pettis, an African-American resident of Marshfield, is murdered and mutilated. C. S. Samuel Jackson, *Oregon Daily Journal* owner, gives Portland the 89-acre Sam Jackson Park. Three Multnomah County commissioners are recalled amid charges of graft and corruption.

1925

The state park system is created. McArthur Court opens at the University of Oregon. The Blue River–Sisters link completes the McKenzie Pass Highway. President

Coolidge declares Central Oregon's Lava Beds a national monument. The Sellwood Bridge opens. St. Mary's Roman Catholic Cathedral is dedicated in Northwest Portland.

1926

Commercial air transportation begins with Pat Patterson's flight from Pearson Field in Vancouver, Washington. The Southern Oregon State Normal School (University) opens in Ashland. The Broadway Theater opens in Portland. The Ross Island and Burnside bridges are completed. The Bridge of the Gods spans the Columbia at Cascade Locks. Multnomah Stadium opens with an Oregon-Washington football game.

1927

Charles Lindbergh flies the *Spirit of St. Louis* to Portland to dedicate the Swan Island airport. The Legislature adopts the western meadowlark as the state bird and "Oregon, My Oregon" as the state song. Fire destroys the college and abbey at Mount Angel. Temple Beth Israel is rebuilt in Northwest Portland.

1928

Multnomah County tries out voting machines. A statue of Abraham Lincoln is dedicated in the South Park Blocks.

1929

The Legislature creates the State Board of Higher Education. Eastern Oregon Normal School opens in La Grande. Blue Bell Potato Chip Company begins chipping away in Portland. The harbor wall on the west bank of the Willamette River is built. Publix Theater (Arlene Schnitzer Concert Hall) opens. Hyster and Riedel International begin operations.

Worried customers gather outside the Northwestern National Bank's Southwest Morrison Street entrance on March 28, 1927, to try to withdraw their money. A run on the bank led to its liquidation.

SIGNS OF ECONOMIC TROUBLE

As the decade drew to a close, Oregonians focused on the economy. Parts of the state were bustling. In Portland, pioneering retailer Fred G. Meyer opened his first store in downtown Portland in 1922. The Iron Fireman, which began producing an automatic coal stoker that same year, was doing $3 million in business by 1927. And other important Oregon companies, such as Jantzen Knitting Mills and Pendleton Woolen Mills, continued to grow. In fact, Portland was among the nation's largest manufacturers of woolen textiles.

But depressed agricultural prices and timber woes hinted at trouble. Several timber mills in the Portland area shut temporarily. Two banks were liquidated: Portland's first, Ladd & Tilton, was sold

CHARLES MCNARY
McNary served as a U.S. senator from 1918 to 1944. A moderate in the 1920s, McNary was the Senate Republican leader for more than ten years and ran unsuccessfully as Wendell Wilkie's running mate in the 1940 presidential election.

and partially liquidated in 1925, and Northwestern National Bank, the city's third largest, in 1927. Unemployment was up. The city added only 500,000 square feet of office space during the 1920s, compared with 2 million square feet after the 1905 Lewis and Clark Exposition. Abbott, the historian, points out that building activity dropped from $38 million in 1925 to less than $15 million in 1929.

Yet even after the October 28-29 stock market crash, civic boosters painted a bright economic picture. "We do not overlook the somber clouds in the background," *The Oregonian* editorialized on January 1, 1930. "[But] that Oregon prosperity will continue throughout 1930 and far into the indefinite future seems as assured as those things can be in a world in which smug prophecy is so often confounded by major surprises in the progress of events."

A transient near the Interstate Bridge in Vancouver, Washington, reflects the tough times circa 1930, when camps for unemployed families grew throughout the region.

Hard Times in the 1930s

THE DEPRESSION TAKES A TOLL ON OREGONIANS, FORCING A NEW RELIANCE ON FEDERAL AID, BUT THE GOVERNMENT JOBS RESULT IN TWO DAMS THAT WILL COME TO DEFINE THE REGION

By R. Gregory Nokes

When researchers arrived at his Columbia River Gorge farm recently, inviting criticism of the construction of the Bonneville Dam, F. L. "Bud" Williams politely sent them packing.

"I guess I disappointed them," he says. But there was no way Williams was going to engage in any revisionist history about the first large Columbia River dam.

Bud Williams appreciates that dam, appreciates the job it gave him during the depths of the Great Depression, and appreciates how it fulfills its purpose of aiding river navigation and providing electrical power. Only 20 when he was hired in 1935, Williams rose to an hourly wage of 75 cents doing electrical work and other odd jobs, a big improvement from the 15 cents he earned as a logger.

"We were all hungry and thankful for having a place to work," he says of the 5,000 men and handful of women who helped build the dam, starting in 1933 and finishing in 1937.

President Franklin D. Roosevelt approved the construction of both the Bonneville and the Grand Coulee Dam in Washington during the Depression to provide jobs for the legions of unemployed in the Northwest. But few developments have shaped the region as have these dams. Together, they provided cheap power for homes and industry, while Bonneville helped open shipping routes to the interior and Grand Coulee's irrigation system turned sagebrush desert into flourishing farmland.

The dams and other Depression-spawned job programs of the 1930s also drew the federal government into the lives of Oregonians as never before, sealing a dependence on Washington, D.C., that continues to this day. The Depression arguably hit Oregon harder than many other states. But there was no doubt about the federal legacy, with Bonneville as a symbol. The federal role, already reflected in the ownership of much of the state's forest and ranch land, emerged in stark contrast to the proud spirit of self-reliance brought by the

BEN HUR LAMPMAN
When Lampman asked "Where to Bury a Dog," Oregonians wondered at their breakfast tables. For 35 years, Lampman's writings drew a loyal following. In 1916, he started for *The Oregonian* as a police reporter earning $25 a week. Lampman went on to become an editorial writer and associate editor, drawing national acclaim, and was named Oregon's poet laureate in 1951.

pioneers who settled Oregon and the rest of the West. But pioneer spirit wasn't putting bread on the table or paying the rent. Portland counted 24,000 unemployed heads of household in 1932 and 40,000 residents receiving welfare assistance, out of a population of about 300,000. In a state of one million, 90,000 were unemployed. Per-capita income plunged from $668 in 1929 to $358 by 1933.

"The state so desperately needed federal money, federal programs, yet it violated the sense of who we were," says Carl Abbott, professor of planning and urban studies at Portland State University. "A lot of the kind of base on which we built the modern state is laid in the 1930s with the federal involvement."

Other national tensions also influenced Oregonians, from the continued discrimination against minorities, to the futile attempts to stamp out alcohol, to the fervor to find cheap entertainment. But the dominant concern was the need for jobs.

DESPERATE TIMES

For many Oregonians who remember it, the Depression stands out as *the* event of the century. It started with a stock market collapse on October 28

Left: *A shantytown built in the Depression, called a "Hooverville," sprouts in Sullivan's Gulch in Portland in 1935.* Right: *Portland alone recorded 24,000 unemployed heads of household in 1932 and 40,000 residents on welfare assistance.*

and 29, 1929, and didn't end until the military buildup at the outbreak of World War II.

Omar Noles, a retired optometrist, was one of the lucky ones. As a 17-year-old, he helped his father at Columbian Optical, a downtown Portland business he would later own. But even working for his father, he was nervous.

"There were always a couple of guys behind you who wanted your job," Noles says. "When they told you to clean up the shop at the end of a week and an 11- or 12-hour day, you didn't say no."

The suffering of others was all around him. His most vivid memory is standing across the street from the American National Bank at Southwest Sixth and Morrison when the state's banks were closed as part of a nationwide "bank holiday" decreed by Roosevelt on March 6, 1933, to help them avoid collapse.

"I watched women banging their purses against those bronze doors and a fellow standing there, and his knuckles were bloody from hitting the bronze doors, yelling, 'I want my money! I've got to pay my rent! I've got to have food.'"

A news story in *The Oregonian* said the "excitement" lasted only a few hours until customers were

LINUS PAULING
Pauling got his start performing chemistry experiments in the basement of his mother's boarding house on Hawthorne Boulevard before going on to Oregon State University. In 1939, in his book *The Nature of the Chemical Bond*, he described the chemical bond that helps atoms stick together to form molecules. That work, the foundation of molecular biology, led, in 1954, to the first of his two Nobel Prizes.

assured that the closings were necessary to safe-guard their deposits.

Many customers at his father's store fell behind in their bills, Noles says, but most tried to pay something when they could.

"In the morning when I used to mop out the store, there would be little envelopes shoved through the keyhole. Some of them contained coins, and once a month you'd receive a dollar bill, maybe. . . . A lot of accounts had to be charged off."

Clusters of shacks sprang up, built by homeless Oregonians and sarcastically called "Hoovervilles" for President Herbert Hoover, Roosevelt's predecessor. The largest stretched from Northeast Grand Avenue to Northeast 21st Avenue in Sullivan's Gulch, now site of the Banfield Freeway.

Monroe Sweetland, a former state legislator, says Oregon was among the most depressed parts of the country, although others argue it was much worse in Eastern industrial states. But even before the stock market crash, the region's chief employer, timber, already was in the tank. By the early 1930s, 80 percent of the region's mills were shut down.

"I think clearly for Oregonians the worst calamity and the most significant event was the Depression, which went on far longer than some places," says Sweetland, a political organizer at the time.

Gordon Dodds, a Portland State University historian, agrees: "The lumber industry was in very bad shape, and agriculture was in bad shape. Oregon was hit very hard."

DEVASTATING FIRES, LABOR STRIKE

The 1930s were a time of turmoil for Oregonians in many other ways. In 1933, one of the nation's largest fires of modern times destroyed 311,000 acres of the Tillamook Forest, the first of three major blazes known collectively as the Tillamook Burn. A fire in Coos County destroyed the town of Bandon in 1936. Fire also demolished Oregon's ornate 1874 Capitol in Salem in 1935; it was replaced three years later with the Capitol that stands today. A longshoremen's strike in 1934 shut down ports in Portland and other West Coast cities for 82 days—the most disruptive work stoppage in the state's history. Lumber and grain exports were brought to a standstill.

Yet amid Depression and disaster, the state continued to build itself. Many of the state's most important cultural institutions took root during the decade: The Portland Art Museum opened in 1932, and the Oregon Shakespeare Festival started its long run in Ashland in 1935. And people took heart from such feats as the University of Oregon "Tall Firs" basketball team winning the national championship in 1939.

Oregon elected its first Jewish governor, independent Julius Meier of the Meier & Frank families, in 1930, and its first woman member of Congress, Nan Wood Honeyman, in 1936. But overall, minorities did not fare well. They were discriminated against socially and, in the case of people of color, restricted to certain neighborhoods: African-Americans largely to the Albina area and Asian-Americans to downtown Portland, north and south of West Burnside Street.

"Realty Board members knew that they would be expelled if they willingly encouraged a minority family to assume residence in a Caucasian neighborhood or apartment complex," wrote historian E. Kimbark MacColl in his 1979 book, *The Growth of a City.*

Courageously breaking the mold was an African-American physician, DeNorval Unthank, who moved

Above: *A 1935 fire in Salem destroyed Oregon's Capitol, which was built in 1874. After a national competition, it was replaced with the current building in 1938.* Top, right: *Fire also raced through Oregon forestland during the Tillamook Burn in August 1933. The fire burned 311,000 acres, and the loss was said to equal the entire amount of U.S. timber cut in 1932.* Bottom, right: *Jobless World War I veterans from Oregon stop in St. Louis en route to the nation's Capital, pleading for promised bonus payments to veterans.*

his family to Ladd's Addition in 1930 despite petitions and vandalism aimed at discouraging him.

The Chinese-American family of Mary Leong lived on Northwest Davis Street beneath a "house of ill repute," with water from an overflowing bathtub occasionally dripping down on her bed. But she was always welcomed when she went upstairs to sell raffle tickets for a school fund-raiser.

"I thought they all looked very friendly, women sitting on men's laps and men sitting on women's laps," recalls Leong. "They always bought tickets."

Ironically, it was the everyday experience with deprivation that blunted the impact of the Depression on her family and neighbors. "Since we were always poor, it didn't make any difference," Leong says. "I had one pair of shoes at a time." But she does remember her father pawning his gold watch for $10 to buy food.

OREGONIANS GET BACK TO WORK

Federally supported projects, large and small, put Oregonians back to work. The projects ranged from the successful Timberline Lodge on Mount Hood to a poorly conceived public market on Portland's Front Street that has since been torn down. Unemployed men found jobs with the Works Progress Administration (WPA), which built Timberline Lodge, while younger men enrolled in the Civilian Conservation Corps (CCC), whose tasks included clearing campgrounds and fighting wildfires.

Fresh out of high school, Webb Harrington found his first job at Mount Hood's Camp Zig Zag, one of 61 CCC camps in Oregon. Housed in military-type barracks, the 200 young men wore uniforms, woke to reveille, and retired to taps. You had to be 18 to 22 years old and poor to qualify for a two-year tour. "It was the first time many of us had a square meal," Harrington says.

Harrington started at the base salary of $30 a month, of which the government sent $25 directly to his widowed mother on their farm in Rainier. The money was sorely needed, as their livestock had been auctioned off at a sheriff's sale to pay their debts. Harrington increased his pay by supervising the commissary and camp store and working at other odd jobs, eventually saving enough to put $150 down for a $1,750 home for his mother on North Houghton Street in Portland. He treasures a

letter of commendation he received from the Vancouver-based commander, then-Brigantine General George C. Marshall.

"Any success I've had in my life I can trace back to my CCC days," says Harrington, who went on to head the Northwest operations of the Coopers and Lybrand accounting firm. "It was one of the greatest breaks I ever had."

ROOSEVELT COMES THROUGH

The Bonneville Dam was the largest of the New Deal projects to put people to work in Oregon, but for a time it looked as if the dam might not be built. Until the mid-1930s, the Columbia was a free-flowing river, challenging to river traffic in the best of times because of its rocks and rapids, and impassable in others. But salmon could swim the length of the river, north to spawning grounds in Canada or east along the Snake River into Idaho.

Roosevelt had signaled a dramatic change in a 1932 campaign speech in Portland when he said the nation's next hydroelectric project should be on the Columbia. After the election, partisans of the two proposed dams, Bonneville and Grand Coulee, fiercely competed for Roosevelt's favor, each assuming only one dam would be built. Public power advocates dominated in Washington State, while private power prevailed in Oregon, a split that continues to this day.

Alarmed when Roosevelt first approved Grand Coulee in 1933, Oregon Senator Charles McNary and Representative Charles Martin staged a sit-in in Roosevelt's outer office in the White House until he heard their last-ditch plea on behalf of Bonneville. As the Senate Republican leader, McNary was not easily dismissed.

Roosevelt agreed on the spot to build Bonneville, too, overruling key aides. He authorized $36 million for Bonneville, in addition to $62 million already approved for Grand Coulee, although the initial project costs grew to $88 million for Bonneville and $300 million for Grand Coulee. Bonneville was completed in 1937 and Grand Coulee in 1941.

Martin, a Democrat who would later become governor, marched around the desk of the president and took his hand, telling him, "Mr. President, you

Above: *The construction of Bonneville Dam spawned 5,000 jobs, starting in 1933 and finishing four years later. President Franklin D. Roosevelt approved the dam to provide Depression-era jobs, but it also would provide cheap power for homes and industry and would open inland shipping routes. Left: Crowds gather to view the plane used by Russian aviators to fly over the North Pole on a history-making flight June 20, 1937, from Moscow to Vancouver, Washington.*

PEOPLE

Population reaches 953,786 in 1930; 51.3 percent live in cities; 2,234 are African-Americans; 4,159 Native Americans live on reservations, and an equal number live elsewhere.

HOME

Average family size is 3.56.

Birth rate increases from 14.1 per 1,000 people in 1930 to 15.6 in 1939.

The Commerce Department finds 6,000 Portlanders live in 1,372 dwellings unfit for human habitation.

A six-room Mount Tabor bungalow on a double lot advertises for $5,500.

Three tins of corn or green beans sell for 43 cents; a pound of economy coffee sells for 29 cents on special; Southern Pacific charges $15 to ride the train from Portland to San Francisco.

WORK

Unemployment in Oregon rises from 25,482 in 1930 to 58,432 in 1937.

Oregon's first claim for unemployment aid is filed in January 1938; eventually 96,741 claims were filed that year.

Farmland increases to more than 2.5 million acres between 1925 and 1930.

Too few jobs

The state's widespread unemployment was reflected in the annual personal income of Oregonians dropping by almost one half over four years.

Source: U.S. Department of Commerce

Personal income

PLAY

More than 7,000 people attend the Multnomah Kennel Club's first dog race in 1933.

The "all talking" picture *True to the Navy*, starring Clara Bow, draws crowds at Paramount in 1930 and costs 25 to 35 cents.

NATIONAL FIRSTS

Timberline Lodge in 1937 is the first building in Oregon constructed by the Works Progress Administration.

BREAKTHROUGHS

Henry F. Phillips Jr. of Portland invents the Phillips recessed-head screw in 1933.

William Gruber of Portland invents the View-Master in 1939.

GETTING AROUND

300,000 cars are registered in 1933.

The State highway system comprises 6,773 miles of roadways; there are 84,920 miles of public roadways today.

First-quarter ridership of buses, trolleys, and streetcars in 1932 falls to 12.9 million passengers from 18 million in 1920.

ENVIRONMENT

A 1930 Oregon Fish Commission survey estimates that half the salmon habitat has disappeared.

SCHOOL

94.6 percent of children 5 to 17 attend school an average of 140.1 days.

Chemawa, a four-year vocational nonreservation tribal school for 750 near Salem, is one of the nation's largest of its kind.

HEALTHCARE

The average daily population of the State Institution for the Feeble Minded hits 840; daily care costs $16.49 a person.

The average daily population of the Oregon State Tuberculosis Hospital is 200; daily care costs $42.28 a person.

CRIME AND JUSTICE

In 1939, Leroy Herschel McCarthy becomes the first man executed in a new gas chamber; *The Oregonian* reports, "It's all done in 45 minutes and costs less than $1."

A skier enjoys Timberline Lodge in 1939. It was built during the Depression to create jobs for unemployed Oregonians.

are following in the footsteps of Thomas Jefferson, and by this act you are sending out a new Lewis and Clark expedition to rediscover the Pacific Northwest."

Critics complained the Northwest didn't need the electricity from one dam, let alone two.

"He [Roosevelt] was in a position to push the dams forward, and the main reason he wanted to push them was to employ people," says Dodds of Portland State. By World War II there were few complaints, as the dams powered the aluminum plants that helped build aircraft that helped win the war.

Salmon and other environmental issues weren't anywhere near the top of considerations when the dams were built. Bonneville was built with a fish ladder, while Grand Coulee was not, blocking Columbia River fish from Central Washington to the river's source in Canada.

"The big economic thing was to help people find jobs because of the Depression," says Sweetland, the former lawmaker. "New industries, barge lines clear to western Idaho, you heard that

DeNorval Unthank
When Dr. Unthank moved into an all-white Portland neighborhood in the 1930s, he was threatened, his home was stoned, and he was offered $1,500 to move. But Unthank said he could not give up, and he went on to co-found the Portland Urban League and was named Citizen of the Year in 1962 and Oregon's Doctor of the Year in 1958.

all the time. They were far more in people's minds than the fortunes of the fish."

A HERO TO MANY

To many Oregonians, Roosevelt was a hero. He carried Oregon in four presidential elections: 1932, 1936, 1940, and 1944.

"He saved the nation," says Magdalen Guild, of Portland, who paid her husband's way through dental school with money from her secretarial job for a group of Bonneville engineers. "I thought he was a great man."

Oregonians who lived through the Depression recall gathering around their old Zenith radios, inspired by Roosevelt's weekly fireside chats. They also vividly remember his crowning visit to Oregon. Harrington won't forget the day Roosevelt drove past Camp Zig Zag in an open touring car after dedicating Timberline Lodge on September 28, 1937, the same day he dedicated Bonneville Dam. Dressed in fresh uniforms, the boys stood at attention along both sides of U.S. 26.

1930

Fire destroys the bank, post office, restaurant, grocery store, and blacksmith shop in Bonanza. Portland Veterans Hospital is dedicated. Julius Meier of Meier & Frank Company, running as an Independent, becomes the state's first Jewish governor.

1931

The Legislature creates the Oregon State Police. The St. Johns Bridge opens. Portland City Council approves a house-numbering system.

1932

Workers complete Owyhee Dam. The first section of the Portland Art Museum opens.

1933

Sparks generated by logging gear in Washington County's Gales Creek watershed ignite the first Tillamook Burn, blackening 311,000 acres of timber. The Portland Public Market on Front Avenue opens. Honeywood Winery begins operations in Salem. The Oregon Coast Highway, U.S. 101, is completed. The Willamette River floods, cresting at 24.9 feet in Portland. Oregon voters repeal the prohibition clause in the constitution. Meier & Frank opens new store at Southwest Sixth Avenue and Morrison Street.

1934

Labor disputes between West Coast longshoremen and shipping companies tie up Portland docks; unrest continues for several years. A strike against the lumber industry idles thousands of workers as long as eight months. In a referendum, voters authorize a tuberculosis hospital in Multnomah County. The Medford *Mail-Tribune* wins a Pulitzer Prize for public service.

1935

Oregon's ornate 1874 Capitol burns in a spectacular fire. Columbia College is renamed the University of Portland. Angus Bowmer founds the Oregon Shakespeare Festival in Ashland. The *City of Portland* streamliner begins service between Portland and Chicago.

1936

SS *Iowa*, a steel freighter owned by States Line, crosses the Columbia Bar in a fierce storm and breaks up on Peacock Spit, killing 34 crewmen. The McCulloch cantilever bridge opens in Coos Bay. Oregon's first congresswoman, Nan Wood Honeyman, goes to Washington, D.C.

1937

President Roosevelt presides at the Timberline Lodge dedication, the same day he flips the switch starting Bonneville Dam. Warner Pacific College opens in Portland.

1938

Governor Charles Martin presides at the dedication of the new Capitol. Voters reject slot machines, the lottery, and a state sales tax to finance old-age pension. Voters appalled by Willamette River water quality prompt the creation of the State Sanitary Authority, now the Department of Environmental Quality. L. S. Crossman finds sandals dating back several thousand years in Lake County's Fort Rock Cave. The new Bureau of Traffic Engineering installs Portland's first traffic lights at Southwest 10th and 11th avenues and Burnside; the first "walk" signals go in at Northeast 37th and 41st avenues and Sandy Boulevard. Congress establishes the Grand Ronde–Siletz Indian Agency.

1939

The second Tillamook Burn chars 200,000 acres that had previously burned, plus 20,000 acres of new timber. The Legislature designates Douglas fir as the state tree. The University of Oregon "Tall Firs" team wins the NCAA Division I basketball championship. Tongue Point is dedicated as the Naval Air Station. Northwest Airlines begins flying out of Portland. *The Oregonian*'s Ronald G. Callvert wins Pulitzer Prize for editorials.

President Franklin Roosevelt speaks in Oregon at the dedication of Timberline Lodge, September 28, 1937.

"You could almost reach out and shake his hand," Harrington says. "With all the Secret Service men now, you could never get that close to the president. But he was just a few feet from us—he could talk to us from the open car."

Bud Williams said he missed Roosevelt at the Bonneville dam, but his admiration for the man caused him to emerge from the Depression as a lifelong Democrat, for which he occasionally takes heat from Republican neighbors. "But I tell everyone, 'If you knew what I went through in the Hoover administration, you'd probably be a Democrat, too.'"

Before hopping "a sidedoor Pullman," as he called it, the Kansas-born Williams said he'd picked corn in central Colorado for 3 cents a bushel, earning 50 cents a day, unable even to afford gloves or socks. He was among the thousands who left the ruined farms of the Dust Bowl and headed West, where there was at least hope of a better life.

PIETRO BELLUSCHI
Perhaps no architect stands taller in Portland history than Belluschi, who designed or consulted on more than 1,000 buildings worldwide. Among his works are the Portland Art Museum, *The Oregonian*, and the former Commonwealth Building.

Williams worked at the dam until 1938, then used the skills he learned to become an electrician. Williams recalls that when the Columbia River was high in the spring during dam construction, salmon would leap up onto a wooden cofferdam, which held back the river while the permanent structure was being built. "We just picked them up and threw them back in," he says.

Williams won't concede that Bonneville harmed the fish—Grand Coulee yes, but not Bonneville. He said as much to the researchers who dropped by recently seeking information about folk singer Woody Guthrie, whose songs about the Columbia River and its dams were sung by Oregon schoolchildren for decades.

The researchers pressed Williams to be critical of the dam. Williams said he doesn't know much about Guthrie, but he knows a lot about the dam, and knows better than to criticize it.

"I think it was wonderful."

Shipyard workers and many of their families gather for a lunchtime launch of another ship at Vancouver Shipyard. The shipyards quickly swelled Portland's population by one-third, drawing 150,000 workers.

At War in the 1940s

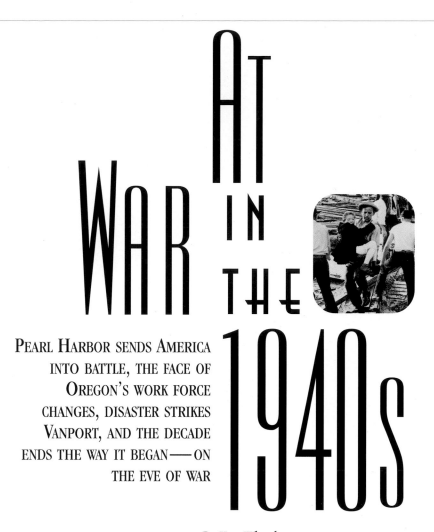

PEARL HARBOR SENDS AMERICA
INTO BATTLE, THE FACE OF
OREGON'S WORK FORCE
CHANGES, DISASTER STRIKES
VANPORT, AND THE DECADE
ENDS THE WAY IT BEGAN — ON
THE EVE OF WAR

By Ken Wheeler

It was the middle of the night, Hazel Stevens of Eagle Creek remembers, when two high school–age boys she knew from the skating rink in Waldport came to the door with a telegram.

"Right then, I knew," she said. "I knew." Eight days after he had landed in Europe, Robert E. Lane, 24, of the 104th Timberwolf Division was killed in Holland. It was October 29, 1944, his daughter Sylvia's second birthday.

Before the war, Robert had worked in the Union Pacific roundhouse in Portland, and he and Hazel, his young wife, had rented a place in Southeast Portland. When war came, she joined her mother in Waldport, and Robert went down and volunteered. One day in Holland he volunteered again, this time to go out and bring in a disabled vehicle, when unexploded ordnance took his life.

"I think the hardest part was when the letters I had written started coming back," Stevens said. "For years, I couldn't celebrate my daughter's birthday on that date."

War was the defining event of the 1940s. And nothing defined it in worse terms than those telegrams so many families received: "The President of the United States regrets to inform you . . ."

The decade began short on hope but became one in which thousands of ordinary people routinely performed heroic feats. The Great Depression still gripped Oregon as well as the rest of the nation as the 1940s began. Nothing, though, ever would be the same once the United States was thrown into the war. Certainly not Oregon, where some have labeled the migration the decade spawned as the "Second Oregon Trail" as workers came to take shipyard jobs. Not only were there jobs, it was a work force with a different face, largely African-American. And now women were wearing pants and carrying lunch buckets, too. Before the 1940s, about 2,000 African-Americans lived in Oregon. By war's end, there were ten times as many, and many of them stayed after the shipyards closed, despite the state's reluctance to move beyond its prejudiced past.

In rural Oregon, things were changing, too. Farmers' sons were off to places called Guadalcanal and Salerno, dots that their mothers tried to find on old maps. Farm laborers came from Mexico to fill the void. Oregon, once so white, so alike, suddenly was different, and the clock would not be turned back.

PEARL HARBOR CHANGES EVERYTHING

The world had been forever changed on that Sunday morning when 353 carrier-launched Japanese planes caught the American fleet napping in Pearl Harbor. A date that would live in infamy: December 7, 1941.

Donald Raymond of Sandy had dropped out of Portland's Edison High School and joined the Navy at 17. Seven months later, he was standing gangway watch on the USS *Sunnadin*, a seagoing tug that was tied up across from Battleship Row. "I heard planes coming in over our stern, and I ran back to see what was going on, and machine-gun fire

Above: *Workers gather for a launching ceremony for the 441-foot* Star of Oregon *at the Oregon Shipbuilding Corporation in St. Johns on September 27, 1941. During and just before World War II, local shipyards produced 1,737 vessels.* Right: *Women shipyard workers such as Mary Carroll at Oregon Shipbuilding circa 1942, helped produce Liberty Ships for the war effort.* Far right: *The Columbia River creates an ice rink east toward Mount Hood on January 2, 1949. In the center of the scene is the Interstate Bridge.*

missed me by about three feet," he recalled. "Pearl was something to remember. I was scared, you betcha I was scared. When the planes came over, I could have hit them with a rock if I'd had one. I saw this one pilot look right at me and grin. Later, they sent three of us to the battleship *California* on grave detail. They had us looking for body parts. We found some."

Ned Voll of Oak Grove was a 20-year-old signalman striker aboard the battleship *Maryland*. "Everything was on fire, and the battleships were all sunk," he said. "Bodies were floating around in the harbor and being picked up by motor launches. It wasn't until Thursday that I got any real sleep or any real food and realized I was scared. I had been so awestruck by the fires and the death. You were surrounded by it."

SHIPYARDS DRAW WORKERS

The war touched everyone and everything, only it treated some more harshly than others. Of singular importance in Oregon, both for the moment and the future, were the shipyards. There were six area yards, the three largest built by Henry J. Kaiser. In January 1941, Kaiser bought 87 acres on the east side of the Willamette River at St. Johns. Eight months later, Oregon Ship launched its first Liberty Ship. The Swan Island yard became known as the Tanker Champion. Escort carriers, attack transports, troop transports, and landing craft slid down the ways at Kaiser's yard in Vancouver, Washington.

The yards recruited workers from throughout the country. In the space of months, Portland's population swelled by one-third with the addition of an estimated 160,000 migrants. Besides the Kaiser yards and their 100,000 workers, the three smaller yards that lined up along the west side of the Willamette employed 50,000.

The world had gone mad and turned topsy-turvy, too. But not everything was different, and Clara Peoples of Portland still clings to some mementos that vouch for that. She was an African-American child of ten when the family left Muskogee, Oklahoma, by train bound for Portland, where her father would work in the shipyards. "Equality wasn't there," Peoples said. "He worked at two yards, Oregon Ship and Vancouver. There was a discrepancy in pay from what the white workers got. But my dad never complained. He worked night and day, six days a week. He was in the union, all right, but it was different. I have some of his old ID cards, and everything has 'temporary' stamped on it."

Still, when the shipyards closed, Peoples and her family did not return to Muskogee as they had planned. "My mother and father talked it over and decided the opportunities were better here," Peoples said.

Hundreds of other African-American families made the same decision. Jaunita Woods-Barnes of Portland planned to return to Oklahoma after her shipyard job ran out but found a husband, who had migrated from Arkansas, and a new home instead.

"There were a lot of jobs blacks couldn't get into," she said. "My husband was a painter, but he couldn't join the union. There were only a few restaurants that a black person could go in and eat. Jolly Joan's was the only restaurant downtown where a black person could go and be comfortable. If you went to a movie, you had to sit in the balcony."

VANPORT'S RISE AND FALL

Both Woods-Barnes and Peoples lived in Vanport, a dike-protected housing project in the flood plain of the Columbia River where Portland International Raceway and Heron Lakes Golf Course now sit. At one time, the ill-fated collection of two-story, 14-apartment buildings housed more than 40,000 people, making the instant shipbuilders' city Oregon's second-largest.

Survivors struggle amid the wreckage of Vanport, a housing project that had become Oregon's second-largest city before flood-waters wiped it out on May 30, 1948.

On December 12, 1942, the first tenants moved in, three months after ground had been broken. Built in a hurry, it came down even faster. It never was intended that the country's largest wartime public housing project, which was plagued by rats, mosquitoes, and cockroaches, would last, but no one foresaw how it would end on another tragic Sunday in the 1940s.

An unusually warm May had overfilled the Columbia River with snowmelt in 1948. Vanport was at the mercy of the dikes that surrounded it, but officials had repeatedly reassured residents. In fact, on May 30, Memorial Day, residents awoke to find a flier under their doors. "Remember," the flier said, "dikes are safe at present. You will be warned if necessary. You will have time to leave. Don't get excited."

It was a pleasant Sunday, the temperature reaching 76 degrees. Vanport was sitting 15 feet below the swollen river's level, but the dikes were holding. Everything would be fine.

At 4:17 that afternoon, things no longer were fine. The railroad dike at the west end of Vanport had been breached. A wall of water, at first ten-feet tall, rushed in. Five and a half years after the first tenant had moved in, Vanport was erased in a matter of minutes.

At the time, Vanport's population of about 18,500 was made up mostly of displaced shipyard workers, returning veterans, and Japanese-Americans who had returned from wartime relocation camps. At least fifteen died, and seven missing people never were found.

Later, some would wonder at what they had chosen to save. "I had just bought a new winter coat on sale at Berg's," said Dorothy Willis, who now lives in Northwest Portland. "It was 90 degrees, but I wore it out of there. We took two suitcases. Had the silverware in one and my husband's work clothes in the other. That's all we had."

Larry Jones, who had come back from the war to live in the Vets section of Vanport, arrived back from a Sunday fishing trip just in time to put his 12-foot driftboat in the water and salvage a few things from his apartment before starting to haul people out. "I grabbed an armload of shoes from my wife's closet," Jones said. "About 20 of them. Later I found there weren't any two alike."

Japanese-Americans board a train in Portland bound for an internment camp. The federal government sent 4,500 Japanese-Americans from Western Oregon to the camps.

Vanport had been Portland's Ellis Island, but now it was gone, its residents homeless and scattered. Floodwaters took the town but not its melting-pot legacy or its place in history as the ramshackle birthplace of Vanport Extension Center, a "temporary" institution that grew to become Portland State University.

The war had made Oregon, particularly Portland, a different place, and there would be no going back. Before Pearl Harbor, the United States always sat with its face toward Europe. No longer. Migration to the war plants of the West had altered the country's balance, and long before the term became popular, the Pacific Rim had a place in the future, and Oregon had a seat in the front row.

FROM NEIGHBORS TO INTERNEES

Not everything about the 1940s saw America at its best. Long after the decade ended, the country wrestled with the guilt of having sent people of Japanese ancestry on the West Coast to internment camps, including more than 4,500 from Western Oregon. Most people of Italian and German ancestry weren't treated that way, but, well, they were white. "I couldn't figure out why we were there," said Ray Shiki of Gresham, whose family was uprooted from its Gresham-area berry and vegetable farm and shipped to the wind-blown, dust-filled Minidoka relocation camp about 50 miles northeast of Twin

HOWARD VOLLUM
Vollum is credited with sparking the growth of Oregon's electronics industry by co-founding Tektronix in 1946. Nearly one-third of his $225 million estate was divided among charities after his death.

JANE POWELL
Born Suzanne Burce, Powell broke into the movies at the age of 14. She appeared in 19 films through 1958, including *Royal Wedding* and *Seven Brides for Seven Brothers.*

Falls, Idaho. "I had grown up among Caucasians and figured I was one of them."

Shiki was 15 when his family was sent to the old Pacific International Livestock and Exhibition Center, now Metro's Exhibition Center. They were held there from May to September of 1942 before being shipped to Idaho. "One of my [Caucasian] friends had a car, and he and about three other friends followed us over there," Shiki said. "We talked through the barbed wire fence, said our farewells. It was a sad one, I'll tell you, and there were some tears."

Mary Minamoto, who now lives in Portland's Laurelhurst neighborhood, was 19 when her family was told to leave the strawberries in the field of its farm at Cornelius. "Later, we were put on a rickety, rickety train to the relocation camp," she said. "On the train, the shades were all drawn, and we couldn't see out. There was this hysteria in the country and people saying, 'A Jap is always a Jap.' On the train, we were all scared. The train made a lot of noise, but everyone just sat quietly and didn't talk."

Immediately after Pearl Harbor, Governor Charles Sprague declared the state a combat zone. Oregonians, especially on the coast, felt vulnerable. There were reports—some accurate, some not—of Japanese submarines off the coast. On the night of June 21, 1942, a Japanese sub did lob numerous 5.5-inch shells at Fort Stevens at the Columbia River mouth, but they all landed in the woods and the sand around the fort. In September of the same year,

PEOPLE

5,223 Native Americans live on reservations.

Oregon's infant mortality rate is 33.2 per 1,000 births, compared with 5.6 in 1996.

The aircraft industry grows from no employees in 1939 to 3,000 in 1943.

HOME

A five-room Colonial in Portland Heights advertises for $3,500; a 100-foot-long westside ranch house advertises for $14,500.

A 10-pound sack of sugar costs 52 cents, four boxes of Oregon strawberries cost 29 cents, and Blue Bell potato chips sell for 15 cents a bag.

A 6.2-cubic-foot Frigidaire sells for $144.95.

Men's washable slacks sell for $2.69 a pair, a sport coat for $12.95.

In 1940, 79 percent of Oregon homes have a radio and 39 percent have a refrigerator.

In 1940, 30 percent of Oregon's homes do not have a flush toilet.

Wood heats 73 percent of Oregon homes in 1940.

WORK

Per capita income is $608 in 1940; it increases to $1,601 by 1949.

Annual jobless rate averages 5.8 percent in 1947–48; rises to 8.3 percent in 1949.

Shipyard employment rises to more than 150,000 in 1943, from 232 workers in 1939.

Jobs draw thousands

Oregon's population boomed in the 1940s, fueled by jobs building ships for the war effort.

1940	1950
1,089,684	1,521,341

Percentage increase: **39.6%**

Population
Millions

- 1,521,341
- World War II
- 413,536

Sources: U.S. Census Bureau and Portland State University Population Center

PLAY

The Portland Art Museum attracts 70,000 visitors with "Masterpieces of French Painting" in 1941.

BREAKTHROUGHS

In 1948, Bud Parsons cables a few Astoria homes, runs an antenna to the Astoria Hotel's roof, and brings three subscribers the nation's first Community Antenna Television; they pick up a broadcast from Seattle's KING-TV.

GETTING AROUND

Oregon issues no license plates between 1942 and 1946 to conserve metal for the war effort.

In 1947, bus tokens sell 11 for $1.

38,355 auto accidents result in 357 deaths in 1940.

In 1940, roundtrip train fare on Union Pacific to the World's Fair in New York is $90 deluxe coach.

SCHOOL

In 1940, median school years completed by men age 25 and older: 8.7; women: 9.7.

WAR

147,633 Oregonians serve in World War II; 4,694 are killed.

Oregon's 41st Infantry was the nation's first division to embark overseas after the declaration of war.

POLITICS

Despite having Oregon Senator Charles McNary on his Republican presidential ticket, Wendell Wilkie loses to Franklin D. Roosevelt in Oregon in 1940.

CRIME AND JUSTICE

The Portland City Club in 1948 issues a report criticizing police for protecting gambling, prostitution, and bootlegging.

A girl amid the debris of confetti on the streets holds up The Oregonian's *declaration of the end of World War II.*

a modified Zero fighter that had been catapulted off a Japanese submarine twice dropped two incendiary bombs in southwestern Oregon in an attempt to ignite forest fires. Neither attack succeeded.

Starting in November 1944, the Japanese launched 6,000 balloons filled with explosives that they hoped the jet stream would carry to the United States. Forty or so balloons, made of mulberry paper and held together by potato paste, made it to Oregon, and one led to the only World War II casualties attributed to enemy action in the continental United States. On May 5, 1945, the Reverend Archie Mitchell, pastor of the Christian and Missionary Alliance Church at Bly in south-central Oregon, and his pregnant wife took five members of their Sunday school class on a picnic and fishing outing. In the woods, the youngsters discovered one of the balloons. Before Mitchell could warn them away, it exploded, killing his wife and the five children.

Willamette Valley farmers made a unique contribution to the war. They planted 20,000 acres of flax, accounting for 95 percent of that fiber grown in the United States. Valley mills spun the flax fiber into linen, which was used, among other things, as the webbing that held bombs in place aboard B-17s.

MINORU YASUI
On March 28, 1942, Yasui, a young Portland lawyer, protested a curfew by breaking it and then surrendering to police. He was jailed for nine months in Portland and then confined in an internment camp. After the war, he practiced law in Denver and finally convinced a U.S. District Court in 1982 to throw out his 1942 conviction. He led the national effort to persuade Congress to pay restitution to those interned during the war.

JAZZ, WAR BONDS, AND 'LANA TURNER'

The war dominated, but there were distractions: big bands and jazz, jitterbuggers and sweater girls. Three shifts of workers kept the shipyards going 24 hours a day. One man's dawn was another man's dusk. There always was a crowd to be entertained. They danced at Cotillion Hall, at McElroy's, at the Golden Canopy Ballroom at Jantzen Beach, at the Up Town and the Mid Town; passed time at the Rialto Pool Hall or one of the many after-hours clubs. Every neighborhood had a theater; Portland's downtown had a nest of them. Bartenders could pour, but they couldn't sell. Patrons had to buy their bottle at a state liquor store, check it at the door, then get it back a drink at a time by purchasing a mix from the bartender.

There was Jolly Joan's, the Pago Pago, the Clover Club, the Cloud Room, the King of Clubs, and the Chicken Coop. The Star was a burlesque theater across West Burnside Street from the nice part of downtown. A time of two-way streets and streetcars with late-night "Owl" runs; a time when

From 1943 to 1958, Portland became one of the nation's hotbeds of bebop and jazz. Separated from the rest of the city by racial prejudice, jazz flourished in a 10-block stretch of North Williams Avenue.

Southwest Fourth Avenue and Taylor Street was the Buttermilk Corner, where a person could get all the buttermilk he could drink for a nickel; a time when shoppers stood and stared at the peanut butter churn that worked tirelessly in the window of the downtown Fred Meyer store on Southwest Sixth Avenue.

But the war, always the war. V-mail and war bonds; air-raid wardens and blackouts; "Loose lips sink ships" and "Kilroy was here"; ration coupons and draft boards; airplane spotters and scrap drives; Lana Turner and Clark Gable selling war bonds from the little stage at the Pioneer Courthouse.

Dorothy Nienstadt of Southeast Portland was one of the 40,000 women who worked in the ship-yards. She went to work for Willamette Iron and Steel in 1942, when she was 21. "Went from making 69 cents an hour to $1.29," she said. "Thought I was rich. They used to have war bond rallies, and I remember one that I went to. If you gave a pint of blood and bought a war bond, Red Skelton would give you an autograph."

For so many, the battles lasted long after the war ended.

WAYNE MORSE
Morse was known as Oregon's "Tiger in the Senate" from 1945 to 1969. The former Oregon law school dean moved from Republican to Independent to Democrat but was unwavering in his outspokenness. He is perhaps best known for his vote against the Gulf of Tonkin resolution, which gave the go-ahead for the Vietnam War. Morse was defeated in 1968 by Bob Packwood, who criticized Morse's anti-war stance.

"My husband would never let me fry chicken in the house," Nienstadt said. "He was on the Franklin (a carrier nearly sunk off Japan), that ship where so many got burned so badly. He said the smell of frying chicken was like burned skin."

It wasn't until about five years ago, said Pat Sullivan of Portland, who was an Army rifleman in such places as New Guinea and the Philippines, that he "quit waking up in the middle of the night screaming."

"My biggest fear was of the dark," he said.

The war. It changed the world, changed America, changed Oregon. It brought terrible endings to some dreams, spawned others.

The G.I. Bill played a significant role in the second half of the 1940s. Stubby barracks-like apartment buildings on closed military bases found new uses on college campuses. Home loans helped fuel the sprawl of one-story tract homes that became suburbs. The baby boom was born.

But one thing didn't change. The 1940s, born on the eve of one war, closed on the eve of another. By the summer of 1950, U.S. troops would be in Korea. By then, though, Oregon had been radically changed, and it would not be going back.

1940

Portland's airport moves from Swan Island to Marine Drive. Republican presidential candidate Wendell Wilkie chooses Oregon Senator Charles McNary as his running mate.

1941

The onset of World War II produces a boom for Portland-Vancouver shipbuilding; more than 150,000 workers will work in the shipyards. Smith Brothers Office Outfitters, Providence Medical Center, and Blue Cross & Blue Shield of Oregon form.

1942

Portland begins a civil defense program. More than 4,500 Japanese-Americans from Western Oregon are sent to internment camps. Mines are laid in the mouth of the Columbia River. A Japanese submarine fires shells at Fort Stevens, but misses. Japanese twice drop incendiary bombs in southwest Oregon in an attempt to ignite forest fires; neither attack succeeds. Camp White in Southern Oregon is dedicated as a training base. Forty-seven Oregon State Hospital patients die and more than 400 become violently ill after an insecticide is mistaken for powdered milk and mixed into scrambled eggs. Oregon State beats Duke 20-16 in the Rose Bowl, which was transplanted to Durham, North Carolina.

1943

Camp Adair in Benton County and Camp Abbot in Central Oregon are dedicated as training bases. Vanport, begun north of Portland in 1942 for shipyard workers, swells to 40,000, making it the second-largest city in Oregon.

1944

Voters approve renaming Marshfield as Coos Bay. Sicks Brewing begins making suds in Salem.

1945

A Japanese balloon bomb filled with hydrogen explodes in Klamath County, killing six people. The Legislature authorizes the Department of Veterans Affairs. The third Tillamook Burn blazes over 200,000 acres of previously burned land and 30,000 new acres. Burns Brothers opens for business.

1946

Vanport Extension Center, the acorn of Portland State University, opens to accommodate veterans eager for college under the G. I. Bill. The Legislature creates the Public Employees Retirement System. Tektronix organizes in Beaverton. The U.S. Supreme Court upholds claims for compensation by descendants of Siletz, Yaquina, Neschisnis, and Alsea tribes.

1947

Governor Earl Snell, Secretary of State Robert S. Farrell Jr., Senate President Marshall E. Cornett, and pilot Cliff Hogue die in a Harney County plane crash; House Speaker John H. Hall becomes governor. The Oregon Institute of Technology opens in Klamath Falls. Freightliner Corporation and Omark Industries form in Portland. The Port of Portland launches the sternwheeler *Portland*.

1948

Heavy spring runoff on the Columbia River leads to flooding that kills at least 15 in Vanport and 32 along the river. 50,000 flee homes (18,500 in Vanport alone); losses run to more than $100 million. Construction begins on the Detroit and Big Cliff dams on the North Santiam River.

1949

Dorothy McCullough Lee, Portland's first woman mayor, embarks on a campaign to rid the city of sin, gambling, crime, and corruption. A moderate earthquake shakes northern Oregon. Dorothea Lensch and Mary Alice Reed-Gardner found the Portland Children's Museum.

Paper scraps cascade from downtown Portland windows during V-J Day, August 15, 1945.

Mrs. America, Cleo Maletis (center) of Cedar Hills, receives flowers from Oregon Governor Elmo Smith and his wife, Dorothy, at a 1957 reception.

GROWING UP IN THE 1950s

 OREGONIANS MOVE TO THE 'BURBS,
BABIES ARE BOOMING,
ELVIS IS STILL IN THE BUILDING,
AND THE AMERICAN DREAM
SEEMS POSSIBLE,
ESPECIALLY IF YOU'RE WHITE

By Spencer Heinz

Cleo and Emma were neighbors, and one day Emma said to Cleo, "I put your name in for Mrs. America."

"You're crazy," Cleo replied. "I've got three kids."

Cleo Maletis was busy raising a family, but it was the 1950s, and anything was possible, and so she ended up cooking and sewing and ironing her way into becoming Mrs. Portland, and then Mrs. Oregon.

A few weeks later in Florida, an astounded but poised Cleo Maletis, 31, was crowned Mrs. America for 1957. She won a $15,000 kitchen and a European tour and moved, with her husband and children, into one of the decade's marketing monuments: their freshly built and nationally promoted "Blue Flame All-Gas Home" in the new

Portland suburb of Cedar Hills. That marriage of Cedar Hills and Mrs. America said much about the nation in the 1950s.

Cedar Hills was one of the hundreds of suburban showcases that churned with a lot of what the 1950s were about. The decade was about a postwar baby boom with one-story starter homes and low-cost loans for grooms and brides in a rush to start their families.

Cleo Maletis was like any other young mother with hopes and fears. But events also made her the symbol of postwar life as it was idealized in the ads: fresh and bright and charmed with possibilities. It was a can-do decade with big-finned autos packed in chrome and the government promise of "expressways" where you could go fast with the kids in the back. The era's last Portland streetcar was yanked in 1950, and it was full throttle ahead in the family car.

Depending on who and where a person was in Oregon, life ranged from impossibly sweet to majestically cruel. So much about it still resonates that often only speaking a word or two—Elvis, Castro, Sputnik, Kerouac, Korea, Rusty Nails, Terry Baker, Mel Renfro, the H-bomb, and saddle shoes—is enough to trigger synaptic yelps of sound and smell.

A varnished box of wire and glass brought it to the living room. Heck Harper, Wayne Morse, and Willie Mays said hello through the rabbit-ear snow. Television became the selling machine for everything from cigarettes to presidents.

Despite the soothing TV images of *Father Knows Best,* stomachs were in knots. The 1950s culture of conformity provided fertile fields of paranoia for U.S. Representative Harold H. Velde, a Republican congressman from Illinois who held communist-hunting hearings in Portland and elsewhere during Senator Joseph McCarthy's campaign of national slander. And in a nation built on ideals of equality, Oregon still slapped down many citizens because of the color of their skin.

"There's one law in history—one big, totally reliable law," says Thomas Vaughan, the Oregon Historical Society director from 1954 to 1989. "And that's the law of irony."

LIFE IN SUBURBIA

For a small place way out West, Oregon packed a punch. It served as sort of a plantation state: Oregon timber, for instance, rumbled to New York to help

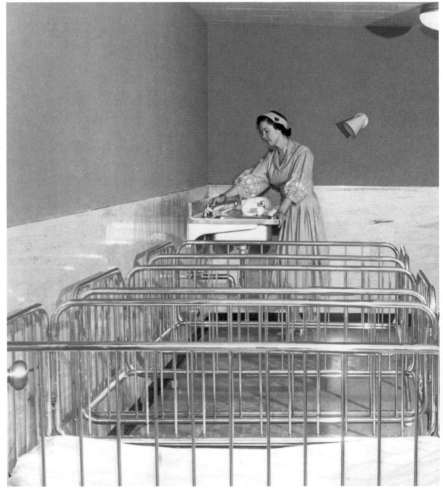

Above: *Mrs. America's home in Cedar Hills reflected the suburban boom in the Portland area in the 1950s.* Left: *This late-1950s view shows a segment of Cedar Hills with Cedar Hills Boulevard on the far left. Cedar Hills held about 2,100 homes by the end of the decade.* Far left: *Portland's new International Airport opened a nursery to handle the increased crowd from the baby boom. The room featured cribs, a baby bathtub, and an around-the-clock attendant.*

85

The Urban League's education efforts help reduce discrimination in Portland restaurants shortly before the Oregon Legislature, in 1953, forbids such discrimination. Here Dick Bogle and his wife at the time, Virlyn, enjoy an evening in Portland's Lipman Wolfe Tea Room.

build thousands of starter homes in Levittown, New York, the biggest subdivision in the nation's history. In fact, Oregon was the top producer of the nation's timber in the1950s, and Cedar Hills snagged plenty as the biggest Oregon showplace for the national housing boom.

From Portland's Council Crest at night, Cedar Hills in the valley beyond looked like a pocket of diamonds. "ONLY $45.00 PER MONTH INCLUDING TAXES AND INSURANCE BUYS THESE $6,750 HOMES," said the flier that real estate agent Wylis Bucher sent around. Bucher's promotional magic helped sell Cedar Hills. He arrived in 1951 and recruited women to a field almost totally dominated by men. "You should be in real estate," he recalls telling schoolteachers, "because you can say things men can't say, like, 'Isn't it darling?'"

Competitors called it "Bucher's harem." He worked the open-house homes in bulldozed fields of forest and soil. The earliest single-family homes sold for as much as $15,000.

Inside, Bucher had set the trap: cookies in the oven with the aroma curling out. That worked sweetly with the news that the government was dispensing loans like candy—getting in for zero down and a

ARTIE WILSON
Wilson helped take Oakland to a 1950 Pacific Coast League pennant and became a Portland favorite with the Beavers in 1955 and 1956. His career also covered play with the Birmingham Black Barons and the New York Giants. Inducted into the Oregon Sports Hall of Fame and the Negro Leagues Hall of Fame, Wilson, now 79, lives in Northeast Portland and sells cars in Gladstone.

100 percent loan if you were a veteran. Then came the flash that the nation's top homemaker was from Oregon, and Bucher pounced on that with another flier: "PORTLAND'S OWN MRS. AMERICA BUILDS HER BLUE-FLAME HOME."

The Maletis family received the suburban lot free, but paid for the brand-new home. About 35,000 people showed up for tours, and Mrs. America walked them through her "New Freedom" kitchen and into a garage fastened to the home itself, an innovation of the era that enabled the auto to be part of the family.

"They even gave her a gardener!" exclaimed one visitor, though that was really her husband, Chris.

Their home became a centerpoint for another bedroom community. The rooms in those homes triggered the baby boom that peaked in 1957. Chris and Cleo Maletis had their fourth child, worked hard, raised a family amid the quiet lawns and trees and breezes of suburbia. The Homeowners Association of Cedar Hills helped keep it bucolic with written restrictions, similar to those in many other subdivisions, against activities that would "detract from its value as a high-class residential district."

Willis Andrews Williams teaches at Failing School. He was among the first African-American educators in Portland, where he was a teacher and vice principal.

And, like nearly everywhere else in Oregon through at least the early 1950s, Cedar Hills Company's restrictions contained this covenant into the 1960s: "No persons except persons who shall be of the Caucasian race shall be allowed to use or occupy said property, or any part thereof, except in the capacity of domestic servants, chauffeurs, or employees of the occupants thereof."

SEPARATE AND UNEQUAL

In other words, the early 1950s were years of opportunity in Oregon unless you were a person of color seeking a home to buy or rent, or a motel room, or simply a place to eat out. Discrimination was legal. Funnels of laws aimed most of Oregon's African-Americans into older and dilapidated areas of inner Northeast Portland.

Dick Bogle, who later became a Portland police officer, a TV anchor, and a city commissioner, remembers scanning ads and racing to at least a dozen apartments and being told at almost every door, "It's already rented."

As a teenager, Bogle was a member of Portland's

OTTO RUTHERFORD
A key figure in African-Americans' push for civil rights in Oregon during the 1950s, Rutherford was president of the Portland chapter of the National Association for the Advancement of Colored People. Both he and his wife, Verdell, cranked out thousands of letters mobilizing citizens, and the Legislature finally passed an anti-discrimination public accommodations law in April 1953.

Washington High School yearbook staff in 1949. He remembers graduating and celebrating with white colleagues. They had dinner and were trying to rent rowboats in Lake Oswego when the line at the lake came to a stop. One of his friends walked back to him with a look of anguish and disgust.

"What's up?" Bogle asked.

"They won't rent to Negroes."

Minnie Belle Johnson, 82, of Northeast Portland remembers traveling as the only nonwhite member of a church caravan, stopping at an Eastern Oregon wayside and having their group turned away.

"Why?" someone asked the waitress.

"Because you have a Negro with you."

Willie Mae Hart of Northeast Portland remembers the beautiful meal she and her sister were served in a downtown restaurant. Then they took a bite—and could not swallow. Their dinners were plugged with salt. Later they paid the bill and heard a crash as they started to go. The waitress had tossed Willie Mae's sister's water glass.

It was not by accident that Oregon was almost totally white. In 1857, Oregon voters had rejected slavery while voting to ban African-Americans from

the state. And a voter referendum threw out a 1950 attempt, by Mayor Dorothy McCullough Lee's Portland City Council, to make it illegal to turn people away on the basis of race.

Change was coming, though. That same year a young Republican named Mark O. Hatfield successfully ran for the Oregon House of Representatives. At 28, he became the then-youngest legislator in state history. A particular memory fueled his fire.

Hatfield had been a student host in Salem to famous singers Marian Anderson and Paul Robeson. Then he heard the news: Hotels in town would not rent them rooms. Young Hatfield was mortified.

About the same time, leaders of Oregon's African-American churches, together with the Urban League and Portlanders Otto and Verdell Rutherford of the National Association for the Advancement of Colored People, were pushing for change. Not lost on anyone was the fact that minorities had fought in the world war, built Portland wartime shipyard boats,

Native American fishermen work the waters at Celilo Falls. The falls, a sacred tribal fishing and gathering site, were flooded by waters backed up by The Dalles Dam, which opened in 1957.

and fought again in Korea. Yet Oregon laws shut them out of postwar dreams.

And not just African-Americans: Oregon Governor Douglas McKay resigned to become the U.S. secretary of the interior and carried out the 1954 congressional termination of 109 Native American tribes, 62 of them from Western Oregon. That led to devastating tribal losses of lands, money, and cultures. And in 1957, The Dalles Dam flooded the historic tribal fishing grounds of Celilo Falls.

African-Americans pushed ahead. Hatfield strategized in their homes. Finally, in a 1953 bill co-sponsored by Hatfield, they broke through the wall. The resulting public accommodations law made it illegal for a restaurant or hotel to turn away a person on the basis of race. Laws alone could not change a century of attitudes. But this was a direct assault on the "Sundown Laws" of many Oregon communities that compelled minorities to be out of town by dusk.

PEOPLE

Population reaches 1,521,341 in 1950: 98.4 percent are white: 5,820 Native Americans.

Baby boom

A baby boom began at the end of World War II and carried over into the 1950s, dwarfing other decades.

Birth rates per 1,000 people

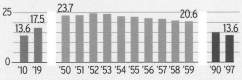

Source: Oregon Health Division, Center for Health Statistics

HOME

In Lake Grove, a four-room home on one acre advertises for $7,500; in Troutdale, a five-room home on 2 1/2 acres is $6,750.

Frozen peas and green beans sell for 19 cents a 10-ounce package; a 6-ounce can of frozen orange juice costs 19 cents; low-fat milk costs 15 cents a quart; and Nescafe Instant Coffee costs 49 cents for a 4-ounce jar.

A Toni doll, complete with curlers, sells for $19.95.

1.85 percent of all babies born in 1950 were to unmarried mothers; by 1959 rate grows to 3.32 percent.

18.4 percent of homes lack a flush toilet in 1950.

WORK

In 1950, work force is 74 percent male and 26 percent female.

Per-capita income grows from $1,657 in 1950 to $2,251 by 1959.

Unemployment rate is 7.1 percent in 1950 and 5 percent in 1959.

Portland ranks 17th in the nation in building permits issued in 1950 with 7,899, but 29th in population.

PLAY

Bend of the River, starring James Stewart, is filmed in Oregon in 1952.

More than 5 million people visit Oregon's 159 state parks in 1950.

Oregon issues 368,000 deer tags and 53,000 elk tags in 1951 and 1952.

GETTING AROUND

In 1951, Oregon's maximum speed limit increases to 55 mph

4,100 people are killed on Oregon's 7,400 miles of roads in the 1950s

In 1950, Oregon has 718,420 licensed autos; "Pacific Wonderland" added to license plates in 1957.

More than 850,000 passengers are recorded at Portland International Airport in 1958; 13.5 million in 1998.

Bus tokens cost five for $1 in 1957.

SCHOOL

In 1952, Oregon has 1,093 elementary and 224 high schools with 304,876 pupils.

In 1959, state college enrollment is 30,484, compared with 16,500 in 1949 and 62,450 today.

NATIONAL FIRSTS

In 1951, Oregon imposes the first statewide laws to control air pollution.

In 1952, Oregon's KPTV is the first UHF commercial television station.

HEALTH CARE

520 cases of polio are reported in 1950 alone; the last reported case of polio occurs in the state in 1983.

WAR

269 Oregonians die in the Korean War between 1950 and 1953.

POLITICS

In 1950, for the first time, more Oregon voters register Democrat than Republican.

CRIME AND JUSTICE

Portland police, accompanied by newspaper reporters, raid eight abortion offices in July 1951.

Governor Robert D. Holmes commutes all death sentences in the late 1950s.

J. Gordon Stuart shows off the $5,000 underground bomb shelter at his home on Halsey Street in Northeast Portland. He later sold the home, and the space now holds a parking lot.

Portland's African-American residents helped carry the new law. They drove 26 cars to the House vote in Salem. The day ended in a blur of tears and smiles. Willie Mae Hart was waiting for an elevator. Two girls from a grade-school class ran to her and wept. They were white, and they hugged her and said they were so sorry about the horrible things that some of the lawmakers had said about African-Americans. Hart said she hugged the little girls back and told them it would be a better tomorrow because of them. Hatfield went on to nearly four decades of public life, yet remembers that day as the most emotional of all.

"It was just a total, spontaneous kind of eruption of joy," he said of the crowd. "I couldn't get to sleep that night."

The next year brought the U.S. Supreme Court's earthshaking declaration, in Brown vs. the Board of Education, that segregation in public education was unconstitutional. And in 1957, with Hatfield serving as Oregon's secretary of state, Oregon passed the

DR. ALBERT STARR
In 1957, Starr was recruited to head a new open-heart surgery program at University of Oregon Medical School. The young cardiac surgeon collaborated with a Portland engineer, Lowell Edwards, to give the world its first successful artificial heart valve in 1960.

State Fair Housing Act, which prohibited the real estate practices that had locked Oregon's African-Americans into poorer parts of Portland.

COLD WAR FEARS

Hatfield's spectacular ascent made him governor by 1959. There was no governor's mansion in those days. Hatfield and his wife, Antoinette, lived on Salem's High Street, and he push-mowed his lawn and waved when drivers honked. He walked to work on sunny days. And he paid attention to the Cold War news: The United States and the Soviet Union had detonated the first hydrogen bombs, and the 1950s came to feature weekly air-raid siren tests.

As a young U.S. Navy officer, Hatfield had arrived in Hiroshima one month after the blast and seen the melted Earth. As governor, Hatfield eventually had a bomb shelter installed beneath his Salem home as a public example. It held water, rations, and two double bunks for his family.

1950

Portland City Council establishes the Portland Intergroup Relations Commission. Nabisco opens North Portland plant. The fourth and final Tillamook Burn strikes.

1951

Completion of an 8,800-foot runway qualifies Portland Airport to become Portland International Airport. Meier & Frank Co. razes Portland Hotel to build a parking garage. Ore-Ida Foods forms in Ontario. Oregon State Penitentiary conditions lead to a strike and reforms.

1952

KPTV, Oregon's first television station and the nation's first commercial UHF station, broadcasts on Channel 27. Senator Wayne Morse bolts the Republican Party to become an Independent, and later a Democrat. Detroit Dam is completed on the North Santiam River. Les Schwab Tire Center wheels out in Prineville. Georgia Pacific begins Oregon operations. Voters pass a constitutional amendment assuring equal representation in the state Legislature. Governor Douglas McKay resigns to become President Eisenhower's secretary of the interior.

1953

The Legislature passes a public accommodations law, making it illegal for a restaurant or hotel to turn away a person on the basis of race. President Eisenhower dedicates McNary Dam. Oregon State's Parker Stadium opens. Precision Castparts begins operations.

1954

The federal government terminates trust relationship with 109 Native American tribes, 62 from Western Oregon; Klamath and Grand Ronde reservations are dissolved. congressional committee holds anti-Communism hearings in Portland. Construction begins on the interstate freeway system: north-south Interstate 5 and east-west Interstate 80-N (now 84). Columbia River bridges open at The Dalles and Umatilla. Oregon City unveils its municipal elevator. KGW-TV broadcasts its first color network program.

1955

The Legislature approves Portland State College degrees. Western Baptist Bible College opens in Salem. Prospectors strike uranium in Lake County.

1956

Republican Governor Paul Patterson dies in office; Elmo Smith succeeds. The U.S. Army Corps of Engineers and city of Arlington agree to relocate the city, much of which will disappear because of John Day Dam. Teledyne Wah Chang forms in Albany.

1957

The Legislature bestows the title "Father of Oregon" on Dr. John McLoughlin and adopts "The Union" as the state motto. The Dalles Dam floods a sacred tribal fishing site, Celilo Falls. Iowa defeats Oregon State 35-19 in the Rose Bowl. Lawmakers pass the State Fair Housing Act, barring practices that had discriminated against African-Americans. *The Oregonian*'s Wallace Turner and William Lambert win the Pulitzer Prize for investigative reporting.

1958

Oregon Museum of Science and Industry opens in Washington Park. New Morrison Bridge opens. Congress designates Lewis and Clark's Fort Clatsop a national memorial. Rodgers Organ sounds its first notes in Hillsboro.

1959

The state observes its 100th anniversary with a 100-day celebration at spruced-up Pacific International Livestock Exposition complex. A truck full of explosives blows up in Roseburg, wiping out several city blocks, and killing 13 people. Construction begins on the $8 million Memorial Coliseum.

Several high school students in 1950 follow Hopalong Cassidy *on an early television set in the lobby of the Astoria Hotel.*

Those subterranean chambers came to symbolize the Sputnik-centered fears of the times. Donna Higgens Mitchell, 45, remembers feeling scared during schooltime duck-and-cover drills and standing as a little girl inside her family's Northeast Portland basement shelter with canned beans and her dolls. She invited friends in, and together they wondered: "What would happen to us?"

In the 1950s, the question of whether to go underground or to evacuate was open to argument. Portland mayors such as Terry D. Schrunk and Fred L. Peterson promoted evacuation plans. In fact, Peterson and Schrunk helped oversee perhaps the nation's most ostentatious H-bomb drill by turning corridors of traffic signals green to see whether people and cars could scram.

They dubbed it "Operation Green Light." After months of rewiring traffic signals under a national spotlight, and under heavy rain at 3:10 P.M. Tuesday, September 27, 1955, sirens wailed, and big-chromed cars jammed getaway roads on cue.

HECK HARPER
Born Hector Flateau on a Wisconsin farm, he was an Oregon TV personality who was handy with a horse and a guitar as Portland's own singing cowboy. Programs included "Heck Harper's Cartoon Corral" and "Circle 8 Hoedown." Kids carried wallet cards identifying themselves as "Ranch Hands"—members of Harper's big fan club.

It was the last great era of unquestioning public trust. While Portland was working at saving lives from outside attack, about 30 miles north of Oregon, the Hanford Nuclear Reservation's H-bomb plutonium production facilities were discharging radioactivity into the Columbia River and over unknowing civilians in the name of protecting those same civilians from the Soviet threat.

The ancient law of irony was immutably in place.

TURNING ON THE TUBE

At 4:30 P.M. on September 20, 1952, Portland gave up the unofficial title of being the biggest city in the United States to have no television station when KPTV became the first Oregon-based station to go on the air.

During those golden years, Friday night wrestling out of Portland's old National Guard Armory featured such TV favorites as Shag Thomas and "Tough" Tony Borne. Now 73, Borne recalls the

Portland's Willamette Heights Owl car makes its last run on February 27, 1950.

time an overwrought patron jumped into the ring and took a swing before Borne jammed his hands into the intruder's pockets and ripped off his pants ("People went nuts"); the feeling of being punched by a tiger ("Almost went to cuckoo land"); and the halcyon days of fighting a 400-pound bear until the Humane Society stepped in and called it cruelty to animals. Retorted Borne: "What about the way that bear treated me?"

Those were the days that created the Oregon of today. Portland's air traffic went from about 400,000 passengers in 1950 to nearly 900,000 in 1960. Planners sketched out potential Portland-area freeways with names such as the Banfield, the Baldock, the Mount Hood. The city bulldozed dozens of blocks in blight-fighting urban renewal projects, and it leveled the magnificent Portland Hotel to make room for a parking garage. Portland took the decade to start to learn that new was not always better.

Oregon's biggest construction project started rising on Portland's east side as the Lloyd Center,

BEVERLY CLEARY
Known for writing humorous fiction for young people, Cleary was born Beverly Atlee Bunn in McMinnville. She created timeless characters such as Ramona Quimby, Ellen Tebbits and Henry Huggins. Her 1950 book *Henry Huggins* was the first of many set around Northeast Portland's Klickitat Street.

which opened in 1960. Portland opened two dozen schools to keep pace with the boom.

Wylis Bucher went on to sell at least 300 new homes in Cedar Hills. It held 2,100 homes by the decade's end, and his piece of Cedar Hills was a steppingstone toward his help with later developments, one of which was Mount Hood's Rippling River Resort, now the Resort at the Mountain.

Cleo and Chris Maletis Jr. raised their four boys in Cedar Hills. Now 76, Chris Maletis is the retired president and chief executive officer of Columbia Distributing and Maletis Beverage.

The couple moved a few years ago, but not far. They live on a rise two miles away.

Today, when the sun goes down, Mrs. America of 1957 still can see the valley of lights where time began with the Blue Flame home and the baby boom.

"I'll tell you," she says emphatically. "It was a wonderful time to live."

Paul McCartney arrives with The Beatles for the group's only stop in Portland, on August 22, 1965. Although teenage fans shrieked at Memorial Coliseum, The Beatles rewarded what they called the most orderly crowd on their U.S. tour with a longer than usual performance.

REBELLING
IN
THE
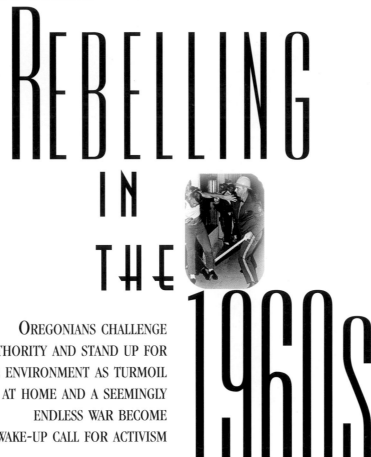
1960s

 OREGONIANS CHALLENGE
AUTHORITY AND STAND UP FOR
THE ENVIRONMENT AS TURMOIL
AT HOME AND A SEEMINGLY
ENDLESS WAR BECOME
A WAKE-UP CALL FOR ACTIVISM

By Steve Mayes

An alarming message came over the intercom: School was dismissed early. No explanation was given. The announcement was unprecedented at South Eugene High School, said Peter Christenson, who got the news in band class.

"We were told we should all go home," he said. "I didn't know what was going on. This was a time when nuclear war was a real possibility."

There would be no bombs, but something deadly was headed toward Oregon. A storm, actually the remnants of Typhoon Freda, had roared ashore in Northern California at midday and turned north toward the Willamette Valley. Anything in its path would endure two explosive hours of chaos.

Prowling Eugene's streets in a Volkswagen Bug, an awestruck 15-year-old

Debris from the Columbus Day storm of October 12, 1962, crushed this car on Northwest Third Avenue near Everett Street. The storm was one of the worst natural disasters in Oregon's history.

Christenson and his friends watched the roof lift off a junior high school, soar over them, then disintegrate. A piece of the flying debris pierced the heart of a 22-year-old graduate student, who died as he covered a broken window in his apartment. Few who were in Oregon that day, October 12, 1962, remember Typhoon Freda. None forgot the Columbus Day storm. Some say it was the worst natural disaster to hit the West Coast since the 1906 San Francisco earthquake. A half-million Northwest households were without electricity. The killer wind claimed 48 lives.

The storm signaled the beginning of an era of expansive social change. The battering Columbus Day winds blew down more timber in just a few hours than Western Oregon loggers harvested in a year. By the end of the decade, it became clear that the timber industry's days as the state's dominant industry were threatened.

On the Capitol grounds, the wind swept a symbol

TERRY BAKER
In 1962, the Oregon State University quarterback became the first football player west of Texas to win the Heisman Trophy. He capped the season with a 6-0 Liberty Bowl victory and a 99-yard touchdown run down an ice-covered field. Baker starred at Portland's Jefferson High, along with future all-pro Mel Renfro.

of pioneer Oregon, a 3½-ton bronze statue of a circuit-riding minister and his horse, from its pedestal. The statue was returned to its perch, but soon the Circuit Rider would be overshadowed by a giant who preached the evangelism of the environment and harnessed a new Oregon activism.

As the 1960s wore on, other squalls swept through sleepy Oregon, generating waves of populism, protest, and political turmoil. Oregon would mirror the national rebellion that led citizens to embrace activism and to question the authority of government.

"You had idealistic youth, affluence, the rise of the drug culture, the sexual revolution, assassinations of national leaders, the anti-war and civil rights movements," said Joe Uris, a leading opponent of the Vietnam War in Oregon and now a history professor at Portland State University. "Put that all together, and what you're bound to produce is an unusual time."

Just before Christmas Day 1964, the Willamette River rose to 48 feet at Oregon City, flooded riverside communities, and forced the evacuation of Salem Memorial Hospital.
Above: Floodwaters rise along Oregon 99 in Corvallis from what was one of the worst Willamette floods since 1890. Left: Flooding from the Willamette River also swept into Wilsonville homes in the December 1964 flood.

DOWNTOWN FROZEN IN TIME

Oregon in the early 1960s was far removed from the Cold War drama playing on the world stage. The state had just celebrated its 100th birthday, but the party paled in comparison with Seattle's 1962 World's Fair and its monumental, 620-foot-tall Space Needle. Downtown Portland was far from today's forest of office towers interspersed with public plazas. Thanks to the Depression, World War II, and the postwar flight to suburbia, downtown Portland appeared to be in a time warp. "If you were to walk through downtown in the early 1960s, you'd feel it was a bit dingy," said Portland historian Carl Abbott. "The buildings you saw in 1962 were the same buildings that were there in 1932."

But these were changing times, and Oregon was shedding its pioneer past. Workers finished Interstate 5 and built the last dam on the Columbia River. Georgia-Pacific Corporation opened its new 28-story Portland headquarters. Community colleges sprouted around the state, bringing affordable higher education to baby boomers. A young entrepreneur named Phil Knight began selling running shoes out of his parents' garage in Southeast Portland.

As a teenage disc jockey, Dave Rogoway observed his generation from a front-row seat. Rogoway worked the night shift at KISN-AM, Portland's dominant rock 'n' roll radio station in the 1960s. The street-level broadcast booth on West Burnside Street was a landmark for teens cruising Broadway.

"Kids back then were a lot less complicated," he said. As the decade wore on, Rogoway said, young people found it harder to be carefree. "The Vietnam War triggered a big change in thinking."

OPPOSITION SLOWLY BUILDS

American combat troops arrived in South Vietnam in 1965. While politicians debated the war, a loosely organized coalition of Oregon students, religious groups, and left-wing political factions formed to oppose it. Peace marches got media attention, but opposition to war also built gradually and quietly in many ways.

"There was a hell of a lot of foment here that may not have had a lot of significance nationally, but it was representative of what was going on nationally," said Uris, then a student activist.

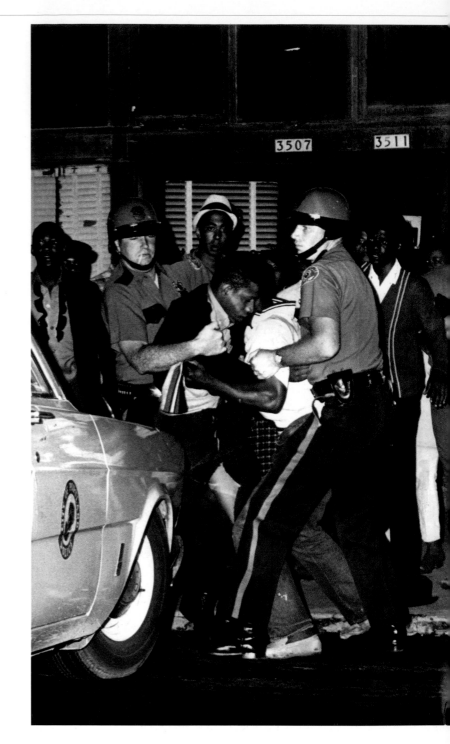

Above: *Portland police respond to a July 1966 disturbance on Northeast Union Avenue (now Martin Luther King Jr. Boulevard). Racial tension would escalate into riots in Portland's African-American community in 1967 and 1969.*

Occasionally, the nation took note. Oregon Senator Wayne Morse was one of the two senators to vote against the 1964 Gulf of Tonkin resolution, which gave President Johnson power to attack North Vietnam without a formal declaration of war.

"Being in the minority never proves that you're wrong. In fact, history is going to record that . . . I voted in the interest of the American people," said Morse, who was unseated by Republican Bob Packwood in 1968.

Baby boomers were coming of age—especially draft age—and found themselves personally connected to the war. Young men left the safe haven of Oregon for Southeast Asia. Fifty-seven thousand Oregonians served in Vietnam, and 799 died or were declared missing in action.

There were almost daily reminders of the far-off war. Protesters at Willamette University would gather to read aloud the names of the American war dead. Newspaper headlines marked the toll: "OREGON MARINE DIES IN COMBAT." "PORTLAND SAILOR LOSES LIFE." "VIETNAM DEAD SWELL MEMORIAL DAY ROLLS."

"We had a kid drop out early in his senior year and join the military, and we had a memorial service [for him] before the year was out," said former state Supreme Court Justice Betty Roberts, then a David Douglas High School teacher.

The war caused Americans to rethink everything. They began to reflect on how the country dealt with issues of race, war, religion, poverty, and pollution—subjects not widely debated in the 1950s. "There were rigid rules and rituals that didn't make sense. People were asking, 'Why this rule, why that rule,'" said Robert Gould, then a war protester. "People were free to be themselves. Suddenly life got complicated."

SEX, DRUGS, AND ROCK 'N' ROLL

The old order was challenged by a counter-culture that encouraged young people to question authority and experiment with mind-altering drugs. A psychedelic scene developed in Portland, with the Crystal Ballroom on West Burnside Street serving briefly as its cultural core. The mix of weird music, light shows, drugs, and kids in funny clothing proved irksome for city leaders. The City Council issued new ordinances that cracked down on runaways, littering, and, in the words of an under-ground newspaper, "excessive public displays of

Left: *Labor Day marked the end of summer vacation and the beginning of riot season in Seaside during the 1960s. More than 125 people were arrested in 1962 when Governor Mark Hatfield called out the National Guard to restore order. Here, Oregon State Police troopers subdue a man in 1963.*

Police stand guard at one of the entrances to the Oregon State Penitentiary, where inmates had seized control of parts of the prison and taken about 40 hostages. The March 1968 riot caused $6 million in damage and injured several inmates and guards. Inmates accomplished a main goal—forcing Superintendent Clarence Gladden to resign.

affection by hippies." The Crystal was cited for a host of building code violations and closed after just 18 months.

It was a time when there was a belief that "sex, drugs, and rock 'n' roll were really the answer to everything," Gould said.

Some did more than party. Activists began to shape an alternative society. They formed food co-ops as substitutes for grocery stores. Homegrown media competed with the mainstream news organizations. KBOO, a listener-supported FM station, went on the air in 1968 with just a 10-watt transmitter. That same year, Michael Wells started the *Willamette Bridge,* an underground weekly newspaper. The *Bridge* connected political factions that otherwise weren't communicating, he said. The paper also became popular, Wells said, with an unlikely group of readers, "parents who were trying to figure out what their kids were up to."

Outside In opened its doors as one of the nation's first free community health clinics in 1968, to serve the hippies and people with drug problems. Portland's small Black Panther Party opened free

KEN KESEY
One of Oregon's best-known authors *(One Flew Over the Cuckoo's Nest, Sometimes a Great Notion),* Kesey was an early promoter of LSD and a founder of the Merry Pranksters, who made psychedelic history as they traveled cross-country smoking marijuana and dropping acid in a Day-Glo-painted school bus.

medical and dental clinics in Albina and organized a free breakfast program for schoolchildren.

"Nobody was paying us a dime. We were doing it from the heart," said Kent Ford, a Black Panther leader. "It was beautiful times back then."

Despite such self-help efforts, job and recreational opportunities were limited for African-American youths. "Things began to fester and fester," said Ford, and that led to small-scale riots in 1967 and 1969. Damage was minimal, unlike the disturbances that left Los Angeles, Detroit, and Newark, New Jersey, ablaze.

For many, involvement in the war protests or the counterculture propelled them to join other causes that gained steam in the 1970s: Native American rights, unionizing migrant laborers, environmentalism. For Holly Hart, it led to a role as a leader in Oregon's gay rights and feminist movements. "Your experience . . . got you used to being an activist and made it easier to use those skills for [other causes]," said Hart, who founded Old Wives' Tales and used the Portland restaurant as a vehicle to assist dozens of local nonprofit groups.

OREGON
LIFE IN THE
1960s

PEOPLE

Population reaches 1,768,687 in 1960; 97.9 percent white, 1 percent African-American, 0.5 percent Native American, 0.3 percent Japanese-American, 0.2 percent Chinese-American.

Portland (372,676), Eugene (50,977), and Salem (49,142) remain largest cities.

62.2 percent of Oregonians live in cities.

HOME

69.3 percent own their home in 1960, the century's highest percentage of home ownership in Oregon.

In 1960, 5.7 percent of Oregonians still have no flush-toilet, and 17.3 percent have no telephone access.

A three-bedroom, two-bath home in Milwaukie sells for $17,950; an English-style, four-bedroom home in Colonial Heights advertises for $13,500.

Gold Medal flour sells 10 pounds for 89 cents; Swans Down cake mix costs 35 cents; 10 jars of Gerber baby food cost 95 cents.

Farmland losses

As cities sprawled and freeways lengthened commutes, Oregonians plowed under farmland as houses sprouted.

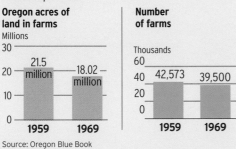

Oregon acres of land in farms
Millions
30
21.5 million — 1959
18.02 million — 1969
0

Number of farms
Thousands
60
42,573 — 1959
39,500 — 1969
0

Source: Oregon Blue Book

WORK

Minimum wage in 1968 is $1.25 an hour for adults and $1 an hour for minors.

Highest unemployment in decade is 1961 at 6.4 percent.

GETTING AROUND

Oregon is one of the first two states to require motorcycle riders to wear helmets, in 1967.

Ten passenger and freight air carriers serve Oregon in 1960.

ENVIRONMENT

Leaks are found in 29 of 180 tanks storing radio-active waste at Hanford Nuclear Reservation.

PLAY

Portland band Paul Revere & the Raiders becomes one of the nation's top bands with "Kicks," "Just Like Me," "Hungry," and "Steppin Out."

Konnie Worth is Portland's first television talk show host, from 1956 to 1968; show spawns Konnie's Klub.

Crowds cheer Portland Buckaroos, who win the first of three Western Hockey League playoff titles in their first season, 1960–61.

SCHOOL

Enrollment in Oregon's elementary schools in 1961 (kindergarten through eighth grade) increases 48.1 percent; high school enrollment, by 60.7 percent.

WAR

57,000 Oregonians serve during the Vietnam War between 1964 and 1973; 799 Oregonians are killed or listed as missing in action.

NATIONAL FIRSTS

In 1962, Oregon's power use per family is highest in the nation, averaging more than 10,000 kilowatt hours a year.

In 1967, Oregon becomes the first state to allow triple-trailers on highways.

POLITICS

Republican Richard Nixon wins Oregon's vote for president but loses the election in 1960.

HEALTH

Heart disease is the leading cause of death in Oregon in 1960; cancer is second.

Oregon's Senator Maurine Neuberger sponsors a 1964 bill to require cigarette packs to carry warning labels; Congress passes a version in 1965.

CRIME AND JUSTICE

In 1962, LeeRoy Sanford McGahuey is the last person executed in Oregon's gas chamber.

Richard Marquette kills and dismembers Joan Rae Caudle in 1961; sentenced to life in prison, he is paroled after 11 years and commits a similar crime in 1975.

Interstate 405, which sliced through the city center, opened in 1969 but hit a dead end in Northwest Portland until the Fremont Bridge was completed in 1973.

Women "had been working on all these other [political] issues, and we realized we've got some issues ourselves," said Gretchen Kafoury, who was elected to the Legislature in the 1970s. The men involved in political campaigns "didn't want to hear about our position on the environment," she said. "They wanted us to make coffee and cookies."

In 1969 there were only five women members of the Legislature. Portland Democrat Betty Roberts was the only woman in the Senate that year—a fact that she was reminded of daily. The 1967 Senate, which was all men, had done away with the women's restroom.

AVERAGE CITIZENS PROTEST

It wasn't just radical left-wingers who challenged the authority of government. Average citizens took on City Hall, as well.

As inconceivable as it might seem today, Portland officials demolished the homes and

WILLIAM STAFFORD
Stafford was a conscientious objector during World War II, and his poems reflected both his pacifism and his love of the Northwest. He wrote more than 50 books, won the National Book Award, and became Oregon's poet laureate. He died in 1993.

businesses of thousands of low-income and minority residents in the 1960s and forced them to relocate, despite community opposition. Big cities were jumping on the urban renewal bulldozer, scraping away decaying areas and recasting them in a modern mold. The first item on Portland's urban renewal agenda was getting rid of a rundown neighborhood of Jewish and Italian immigrants on downtown's southern edge. Opponents tried in vain to stop the project, but they were loosely organized and poorly financed.

"They wiped out a whole neighborhood. You'd never do that today," said Donald J. Sterling Jr., the late editor of the now-defunct *Oregon Journal.*

There was little opponents could do to derail the projects, said Oliver Norville, an attorney who represented the Portland Development Commission, the city's urban renewal agency. But by the end of the decade, neighborhood activists had honed their skills and blocked urban renewal around Good Samaritan Hospital and the Lair Hill neighborhood, just south of downtown. In the 1970s, neighborhood

Memorial Coliseum opened November 3, 1960, but was little more than a roof in late 1959. The coliseum opened with a performance of "Holiday on Ice," but would become home to the Trail Blazers and the Portland Buckaroos and Winter Hawks ice hockey teams.

associations became part of the city government. They were no longer fighting City Hall; they were part of City Hall.

ECONOMY IN TRANSITION

The state's strong economy, powered by the one-two punch of timber and agriculture, freed Oregonians to focus on social issues. But it was a precarious prosperity. An increase in interest rates or a slack demand for new homes could spell trouble for Oregon.

Although it received little attention in the 1960s, the timber industry was headed for changes.

"What seemed like a boom decade was actually a transition period," said William Robbins, an Oregon State University historian. "It still seemed boundless, but there was an awareness that it couldn't go on forever."

Privately, forestry experts and industry leaders realized timber companies were harvesting their trees too quickly, and the time would come when

DON SCHOLLANDER
The Lake Oswego athlete became the first swimmer to win four gold medals at a single Olympics, in Tokyo in 1964. He won another gold and a silver medal in the 1968 Olympics.

demand outstripped supply. But few were criticizing the practices.

"[Environmentalists] had not come to strength yet, and they weren't bothering us any," said Loran L. "Stub" Stewart, former president of Bohemia, a Eugene lumber company.

But one man could see clearly that Oregon had paid a steep price for its economic progress.

ENVIRONMENTALISTS EMERGE

A documentary produced by a Portland newsman and unsuccessful politician aired on KGW-TV on November 21, 1962. *Pollution in Paradise* chronicled the lethal effects of sewage and toxic waste that had flowed into the Willamette River for decades. The program ignited public outrage, and the Legislature responded by giving the state power to shut down corporate polluters. It also helped spark Oregon's environmental movement and launch the political career of the reporter, Tom McCall.

1960

Maurine Neuberger is elected Oregon's first woman senator, the nation's third. Memorial Coliseum opens. Dr. Albert Starr implants a replacement for the mitral heart valve developed with Lowell Edwards; in 1963, Starr performs triple valve replacement. Evergreen International Aviation is founded in McMinnville.

1961

The Legislature designates chinook salmon as the state's official fish. Dammasch State Hospital opens in Wilsonville. Portland Community College is founded. Interstate 5 is completed between Portland and Salem. Arlington gets dial telephone service.

1962

The October 12 Columbus Day storm (winds 170 mph at Mount Hebo, 116 mph in Portland) rips through Western Oregon, killing 48. The Legislature creates the Oregon Tax Court. Oregon Regional Primate Center opens in Washington County. Packy is the first elephant born at the Portland Zoo. Governor Mark Hatfield calls out the National Guard to quell youth violence in Seaside during Labor Day weekend.

1963

The Legislature creates the Otter Trawl Commission. Hillcrest Vineyard forms in Roseburg.

1964

Cougar Dam on the South Fork of the McKenzie River and Round Butte Dam on the Deschutes River are completed. Voters repeal the state's death penalty. Wayne Morse is one of two U.S. senators to oppose the Gulf of Tonkin resolution. Blue Ribbon Sports, which will evolve into Nike Inc., forms. Portland buys Henry Pittock Mansion. Portland Opera Association is founded. Oregon Women's Correctional Center opens in Salem. Japan-America Society organizes.

1965

The Legislature designates the thunderegg as the state rock. Michigan pelts Oregon State 34-7 in the Rose Bowl. Port of Portland takes delivery on the dredge *Oregon*. The Oregon Historical Society lays cornerstone for a library-museum complex.

1966

Archbishop Edward D. Howard retires at 89 after leading the Archdiocese of Portland for more than 40 years. Four-mile Astoria Bridge opens at the mouth of Columbia. Interstate 5 is completed between Washington and California. Oregon Graduate Center opens in Beaverton. Mount Hood, Clackamas, and Linn-Benton community colleges are founded. Petroglyphs are discovered under Willamette Falls. Larry Mahan of Brooks wins pro rodeo circuit's all-around championship; he will win the next four years and again in 1973.

1967

Legislature passes and Governor Tom McCall signs the Oregon Beach Bill, guaranteeing public use of state's dry sand beaches. Multnomah County adopts its home-rule charter. Portland buys Multnomah Stadium.

1968

Vice President Hubert Humphrey dedicates John Day Dam, the final megadam on the Columbia. Assassination of civil rights leader Martin Luther King Jr. prompts demonstrations in Portland. Prisoners riot at Oregon State Penitentiary. Applying the "Fosbury Flop," Medford's Dick Fosbury wins the high jump gold medal at the Mexico City Olympics. Bob Packwood ends Wayne Morse's 24-year Senate reign.

1969

The Legislature creates the Court of Appeals, Department of Environmental Quality, Executive Department, and Department of Transportation, and makes the American beaver the state animal. American State Bank, the state's first African-American–owned bank, opens. Oregon Bach Festival starts in Eugene. Albina district erupts after a confrontation between police and 150 youths at a drive-in restaurant; more than 100 are arrested, and at least 20 fires set. Portland State College becomes Portland State University.

Japanese Crown Prince Akihito and Princess Michiko tour Lloyd Center's Meier & Frank store in 1960 with Governor Mark Hatfield. Lloyd Center was the world's largest shopping center when it opened that year.

Pollution and poisons were receiving national scrutiny. Biologist Rachel Carson's book *Silent Spring,* an account of the lethal effect of manmade chemicals and pesticides such as DDT, had just been published.

Oregonians certainly had reason to worry about their environment. From 1940 to 1970, metropolitan Portland's population doubled. In the mid-1950s, the Willamette Valley had 2.8 million acres of flat farmland. Within 15 years, developers gobbled up 500,000 acres—almost 20 percent. Oregonians found themselves crowded out of their own state campgrounds, mainly by Californians. Oregonians were advised not to drink, swim, or fish in the Willamette River because it had become an industrial toilet. Exhaust from automobiles and the burning of agricultural and timber mill waste polluted the air.

The time was ripe for McCall, a liberal Republican who once ran for Congress and had worked in state government, to jump back into politics. McCall was elected secretary of state in 1964 and ran for governor in 1966. For the first time, "livability" dominated the governor's race.

REV. JOHN JACKSON
After arriving as pastor of Olivet Baptist Church in 1964, Jackson moved to the front lines of the push for civil rights. He helped found the Black United Front, led a boycott of Portland Public Schools, and demonstrated against apartheid. And yet establishment leaders, including Portland's mayors, routinely sought his counsel. He died in 1994.

The charismatic McCall easily defeated Democrat Bob Straub and immediately led the charge to clean up the Willamette and protect the state's air, water, and land. "Oregon . . . enforces to the hilt an 11th commandment: Thou shall not pollute," the 6-foot-5 McCall thundered. Under McCall, corporate polluters faced tough new pollution regulations if they wanted to stay in business.

When a Cannon Beach motel owner fenced off part of the beach for its guests, thousands of angry letters and calls flooded the Capitol, demanding preservation of Oregon's open beaches. McCall used the outrage and his political instincts to literally draw a line in the sand separating public and private property and forced a reluctant Republican-controlled Legislature to pass the so-called Beach Bill to protect public access.

"When you live in Oregon, you realize how carefully the public watches its heritage. Let any speculator attempt to move in the shadows, and the voice of the people thunders through the governmental halls," McCall said. "Oregonians care very deeply about the Oregon country. And this is a good thing."

Governor Tom McCall and Secretary of State Clay Myers promote Oregon's bottle bill, the nation's first law requiring deposits on pop and beer containers.

BLAZING TRAILS IN THE 1970s

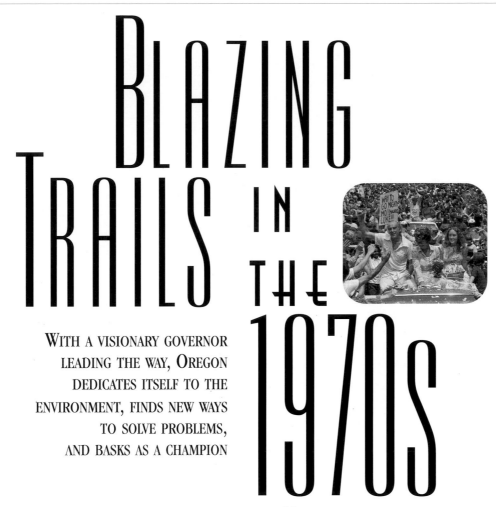

WITH A VISIONARY GOVERNOR LEADING THE WAY, OREGON DEDICATES ITSELF TO THE ENVIRONMENT, FINDS NEW WAYS TO SOLVE PROBLEMS, AND BASKS AS A CHAMPION

By Brent Walth

You could walk into many stores in Oregon during the 1970s and find the perfect greeting card to send out-of-staters.

"Tom Lawson McCall, governor," read a typical card, "on behalf of the citizens of the great state of Oregon, cordially invites you to visit . . . Washington or California or Idaho or Nevada or Afghanistan."

This and other Oregon "ungreeting cards" ("People in Oregon don't tan in the summertime; they rust," read another) summed up all the pride and self-satisfaction that typified Oregon in the 1970s. For decades, the nation thought of Oregon as that state just north of California, a place filled with lumberjacks and soaked by rain. No longer. In the 1970s, Oregon redefined itself as a progressive place with an unlimited

Crews pour concrete in October 1977 on what would become Portland's Downtown Transit Mall. The mall became a cornerstone of Mayor Neil Goldschmidt's vision for protecting downtown Portland from urban decay.

imagination for solving the social ills plaguing other places. Oregon in this decade put livability above all else.

Today, the 1970s shimmer in the state's memory. It was an era in which Oregon seemed to do everything right. Looking back now, how much of that time, the cradle of the vaunted "Oregon Story," was just myth? A good deal of it, to be sure. But at the time, the nation believed. And so did Oregonians. The 1970s brought a civic momentum in Oregon, and a state conceit. We've never really gotten over the feeling. And no leader since has been able to make us feel the same way or shake the shadow of the man who made it all possible.

Oregon's decade of the 1970s lasted eight years, nine months, and 28 days. The era began January 12, 1971, when Governor Tom McCall appeared on national television and told people to stay out of his state. Well, McCall didn't really say that. And he spent

PAUL WALDSCHMIDT
In 39 years in Oregon, 16 as president of the University of Portland, Waldschmidt marched for civil rights, helped establish what is now the Ecumenical Ministries, and helped provide housing, jobs, and language training for 10,000 refugees, most from Southeast Asia. He died in 1994.

years untangling the message he sent to the world that night.

As McCall prepared to start his second term as Oregon's governor, CBS correspondent Terry Drinkwater asked him to sum up his views on conservation, which had already made him famous.

"Come visit us again and again," McCall said for Drinkwater's national audience. "But for heaven's sake, don't come here to live."

McCall's statement was more than a quip. He had made protection of Oregon's environment and livability the hallmark of his work. He was most concerned about uncontrolled growth. He had seen Oregon's population of 1.7 million in 1960 grow to 2 million 10 years later, and he believed predictions that the rate would increase. Thousands of acres of farmland around cities had been tilled under for subdivisions, often without regard to how city services or roads would serve them.

The statement—shortened and made famous as "Visit, but don't stay"—was McCall's warning

Governor Tom McCall serves a crowd of children ice cream at a Keizer school event promoting keeping Oregon "Green, Clean and Beautiful." The charismatic governor who emphasized the environment also drew national attention.

that any place, and especially Oregon, stood to lose its precious livability if it did not prepare for growth and erect tough environmental standards.

DEQ VS. BOISE CASCADE

No scene better symbolized Oregon's determination to protect its environment in the 1970s than the confrontation between Boise Cascade and the young, robust Oregon Department of Environmental Quality. The DEQ warned Boise Cascade that miscreant air pollution from its Salem paper mill had to end. So in July 1972 the company shut the mill down. Hundreds of angry workers marched on the Capitol to protest, only to find Governor McCall and his fierce DEQ chief, L. B. Day, there to meet them. Unable to bully the state, Boise Cascade agreed to clean up its stacks and reopen the mill.

McCall's tough stands and "Visit, but don't stay" message struck concern among Oregon's business

BILL NAITO
With his brother, Sam, Naito built a $140 million retail and real estate empire that included the Made In Oregon stores and the Galleria mall. But it was Bill Naito's public vision for improving Portland and his business boldness that won him acclaim and affection.

leaders. Some feared an environmental hysteria would make the state inhospitable to new business. Georgia-Pacific Corporation Chairman Robert Pamplin Sr. in 1971 blasted the thinking as that of "woodsy witch doctors of a revived nature cult."

Oregon indeed might lose some businesses, McCall fired back. "Industry must come here on our terms," he replied to critics, "play the game by our environmental rules, and be members of the Oregon family."

An Oregon family. What leader had ever spoken that way before? With his bravado and wit, McCall massaged the state's self-image.

Oregonians became so enamored of their own that they could laugh at their isolationist image, and not just with Oregon ungreeting cards. Popular commercials for Portland's Blitz-Weinhard beer featured an Oregon Border Patrol officer who repeatedly stops a California brewery from trucking its Schludwiller beer into the state. "Well, now," the patrolman would ask, "where you going with all that beer?" before sending the Schludwiller truck back over the state line.

Economic strength gave McCall and Oregon the license to be choosy about the kind of growth the state welcomed. The timber industry stoked the fire in Oregon's boilers. In the 1970s, nearly one of every eight jobs was tied to the timber industry, and the nation's demand for new houses kept it burning. By 1978, the annual per-capita income in Oregon hit $8,078, surpassing the national average. You could earn more here, where it also cost less to live. Why not be smug?

MAKING THE FUTURE WORK

With a booming economy, the Oregon Legislature rarely worried about balancing the state budget. Instead, lawmakers used their time thinking about how to fix social problems. In the 1970s, law-makers decriminalized marijuana, passed a raft of consumer protection legislation, and introduced the most ingenious anti-littering law in the nation, the bottle bill.

This law symbolized the openness of Oregon government: A lone Salem salesman, Richard Chambers, a man without clout or connections, worked to pass it. A single citizen could still make a difference.

Yet, no law passed during the decade changed the course of Oregon more than Senate Bill 100 in the 1973 Legislature. The law required that every city and county tell the state how it would plan for growth. Oregon became the first state to require land-use planning, a concept few people then understood. A tiny but well-financed activist group, 1000 Friends of Oregon, used the courts to set one precedent after another to aim the new law toward as much conservation as was possible. Opponents went to the ballot in 1976 and 1978 with measures seeking to dismantle land-use laws. Voters trounced the measures.

The population breather McCall had hoped for, however, never came. Instead, his statement might have backfired. Oregon population in the 1970s grew twice as fast as it had during the 1960s, hitting 2.63 million by decade's end. And why not? McCall had given the state an allure, a mystery. Cities such as Eugene, for example, shined idyllically. Hailed as the running capital of the world—thanks largely to the fame of a University of Oregon track hero,

Steve Prefontaine, Eugene laced its streets and river-front with bike paths and running trails.

The national media turned their spotlights on Oregon, speaking of the state in reverent tones. In the 1970s, so much else happening in the United States had shaken Americans' faith: gasoline shortages, a draining war in Asia, a felonious presidency. Oregon appeared to have figured out a better way; *Newsweek* magazine in 1973 even described the state as the place "where the future works."

Why wouldn't everyone want to live there?

GOLDSCHMIDT'S VISION

The ability to see into the future looked strongest in Portland, the state's largest city. In 1970, you could stroll downtown to shop at J.C. Penney's or Rhodes or Lipman Wolfe department stores. But as suburban malls such as Washington Square and Jantzen Beach Center sprang up, downtown Portland faced the possibility of decay that had gnawed at other big cities. To match the state's activist governor, the city reversed 16 taciturn years under Mayor Terry Schrunk with a jolt, electing Neil Goldschmidt.

Goldschmidt had worked his way up to the Portland City Council through neighborhood activism. He saw that avoiding downtown rot meant welcoming people downtown, and more cars didn't necessarily figure into the plans. Across the city, neighborhood groups had risen up against proposed freeways, just as the state's long interstate-building campaign headed for its finale. Interstate 205 eventually ran around the city's east side to span the Columbia. In 1973, cables pulled the long span of the Fremont Bridge up from barges and into place, connecting the deep Interstate 405 gash through downtown. The early 1970s included plans for an Interstate 505 through Northwest Portland, and another bypass, called the Mount Hood Freeway, to run east from Interstate 5's Marquam Bridge six miles to Southeast 96th Avenue.

Goldschmidt gave heed to grassroots groups, including Sensible Transportation Options for People, which warned against eviscerating Southeast Portland neighborhoods for the Mount Hood Freeway. Other Portland leaders, including City Commissioner Lloyd Anderson, suggested using

Above: *Workers completed the Fremont Bridge, but Portland Mayor Neil Goldschmidt put a stop to more freeways. In March 1973, hydraulic jacks lift this 902-foot-long, 6,000-ton center span of the Fremont Bridge, a technological feat that drew engineers from all over the world.* Left: *Goldschmidt leads a group of cyclists as they bike to work as part of Bicycle Commuter Day in May 1978. Goldschmidt didn't think the key to downtown revival was necessarily more cars.*

Above: *Trail Blazers coach Jack Ramsay celebrates with thousands of fans in downtown Portland on June 6, 1977, after his team beat the Philadelphia 76ers for the city's first National Basketball Association championship.*

federal money for mass transit instead. The prospect of passing up millions of dollars from the federal government to build the freeways seemed crazy to Portland's power elite. "If the [Mount Hood Freeway] should be abruptly abandoned by the core city," warned *The Oregonian* in an editorial, "it would certainly bring chaos to transportation planning, not only in the city, but in this entire part of the state."

Far from bringing chaos, Goldschmidt forged a regional transportation vision, which produced the Downtown Transit Mall and, somewhat as an afterthought for the Mount Hood Freeway, a light-rail system. The transportation ideal Goldschmidt introduced remains the reigning agenda in the region today.

A CITY OF CHAMPIONS

The perfect coda to a prideful era in Portland and Oregon came not amid public policy decisions but on the wooden basketball court in Memorial Coliseum, delivered when a coach named Jack Ramsay took control of the hapless Portland Trail Blazers. In its six years, Portland's only major-

DAVID SOHAPPY SR. Sohappy, a Wanapum who believed salmon fishing was an exercise of his treaty rights, preserved tribal fishing along the Columbia River. A landmark 1968 federal court ruling said states could regulate tribal treaty fishing only for conservation purposes. That ruling led to the 1973 Boldt decision, which guaranteed the four Columbia River treaty tribes half the river's salmon catch.

league sports franchise had never had a winning season. Ramsay remade the team around its towering Redwood center, the injury-prone Deadhead, Bill Walton.

Behind Walton and the fast break, the Trail Blazers went to the playoffs for the first time and, as underdogs, beat the Chicago Bulls, ground down the Denver Nuggets, and swept the favored Los Angeles Lakers. A fever called Blazermania heated the city.

On Sunday June 5, 1977, before 12,951 people in Memorial Coliseum, in Game 6 of the NBA Finals, the Blazers clung to a 109-107 lead. With two seconds left, Philadelphia 76er forward George McGinnis took a jump shot to tie the game. The ball fell short, hit the rim, and Walton ascended to meet it. When he batted the rebound into the arms of Blazer guard Johnny Davis, the city erupted. Thousands filled Portland's streets for an all-night celebration.

The next day, tens of thousands more clogged downtown Portland for a parade honoring the team. Walton tried to ride his bike through the parade before abandoning it when the enthusiastic crowds mobbed him.

Youths flock to Vortex, the nation's first state-sanctioned rock festival, held at McIver Park near Estacada in September 1970. The event was Governor Tom McCall's ingenious way of diffusing potential friction between youthful anti–Vietnam War protesters and the 20,000 "love-it-or-leave-it" American Legionnaires visiting Portland that same weekend for a national convention.

PEOPLE

Population in 1970 hits 2,091,385; 97.2 percent white.

In 1970, 8.2 percent of births in Oregon are to unmarried mothers; by 1979, it increases to 13.5 percent.

"Tourists" stay

Despite entreaties for tourists to visit, but not stay, Oregon experienced another boom in population. The '70s was the third-fastest growing decade of the century, behind the 1900s and 1940s.

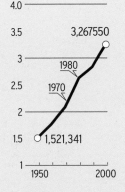

1970	1980
2,091,533	2,633,156

Percentage increase:
25.9%

Source: U.S. Census Bureau

WORK

In 1970, Oregonians earn an average of $3,914; by 1978, that jumps to $8,078.

In 1974, the minimum wage is $1.60 an hour; it rises to $2.65 by 1979.

1975 sees Oregon's then-highest unemployment rate, 10.6 percent, since records first were kept in 1947.

HOME

A three-bedroom, 1²⁄₃-bath home in Southeast Portland sells for $26,000; a 16-year-old, four-bedroom home near Madison High School sells for $15,600; a 2-year-old, four-bedroom home in Raleigh Hills on a 100-by-100-foot lot sells for $34,950.

Pork chops sell for 79 cents a pound; 12 6-ounce cans of frozen pink lemonade go on special for $1; Chiquita bananas cost 12 cents a pound; a half gallon of ice cream costs 59 cents.

In 1970, 11.1 percent of Oregonians have no telephone; 3.6 percent lack complete plumbing.

GETTING AROUND

Governor Tom McCall invents the odd-even calendar-day system for purchasing gasoline during the 1973-74 gas shortage.

To save fuel, Oregon is the first state to implement a 55-mph speed limit.

ENVIRONMENT

Portland imposes a limit on downtown parking in 1975 because the city violates federal air-quality standards for carbon monoxide 50 times.

The Environmental Protection Agency declares Portland the most livable city in 1975.

SCHOOL

Public school enrollment grows to 498,469 in 1970-71, rising from 409,900 in 1960.

Colegio Cesar Chavez is founded in Mount Angel in 1973; it will close in 1982.

PLAY

In 1971, Oregon issues 1.4 million fishing and hunting licenses, rising from 353,000 in 1950.

Portland's Saturday Market begins in 1974.

Oregon City residents Mike Marshall and John Stalberger Jr. invent Hacky Sack and sell more than a million footbags by 1983.

Filmmakers shoot *Animal House* in Eugene, *The Shining* at Timberline, *One Flew Over the Cuckoo's Nest* in Salem, *Rooster Cogburn* in Bend, and *Kansas City Bomber* in Portland in the 1970s.

WAR

57,000 Oregonians serve during the Vietnam War between 1964 and 1973; 799 Oregonians are killed or missing in action.

POLITICS

Republican Richard Nixon wins Oregon in 1972; Republican Gerald Ford edges Jimmy Carter in Oregon in 1976.

CRIME AND JUSTICE

Greta Rideout is the first woman in the nation to accuse her husband of rape while they were still living together; John Rideout is acquitted in 1978.

During the 1970s, there are 1,089 murders; from 1990 to 1998, Oregon had 1,130 murders.

Portland police equipped with 42-inch-long clubs prepare to break up a Vietnam War protest in the South Park Blocks, in May 1970. The confrontation turned bloody, and dozens were injured. The deaths of four Kent State University students in Ohio had escalated anti-war fervor at Portland State University, prompting PSU's president to shut down the campus for a week.

POWER AND TIMBER PROBLEMS

The 1970s in Oregon brought a period of riches, of economic wealth, of ideas, of fame. But there was scarcity, too. And the shortages that haunted the 1970s left wounds that still ache. In 1973, the Northwest's famous rain did not come as it had in the past, and reservoirs went dry behind the giant federal dams that generated the electricity for the region. The Bonneville Power Administration predicted brownouts, which never came. Still, the scare allowed BPA and the region's power companies to promote nuclear power.

Portland General Electric, already building its Trojan Nuclear Plant along the Columbia River 40 miles north of Portland, promised to use the new plant to close the Northwest's "generation gap," as one of the utility's ads put it. In the mid-1970s, public utility districts in Oregon got behind a

STEVE PREFONTAINE
In life, track legend Prefontaine brought charisma and talent to long-distance running. The University of Oregon prodigy from Coos Bay broke 14 U.S. records. In death, he became a sports folk hero. Within hours of running his last race, 24-year-old Prefontaine was dead, pinned under his car after it slammed into a rock wall in Eugene.

massive plan by the Washington Public Power Supply System (WPPSS) to build five nuclear plants.

The legacy triggered by fears of scarcity remains a financial drain. Trojan ran just 17 years of its predicted 40-year life span, and PGE ratepayers still pay for it. But at least it ran. WPPSS, better known as "Whoops," spent more than $6 billion and finished only one of the five plants before committing the biggest municipal bond default in history. Oregon ratepayers still pay for those plants, too.

But the greatest scarcity, the one that would leave the deepest scars on Oregon, came in the state's fabled woods. For years, the timber industry had swung its saw and shaved one hill after another until the supply of trees dwindled. With timber supplies running low on private lands, the timber industry and Oregon's congressional delegation flung open the U.S. national forest reserves. Dependence on public logs grew, but the supply

NEWSREEL

1970

The American Legion holds its national convention in Portland; the prospect of anti-war demonstrations inspires Governor Tom McCall's Vortex, the nation's first and perhaps only state-sanctioned rock festival. Voters approve the Scenic Waterways Act, a landmark initiative aimed at preserving lakes and streams. Portland wins a National Basketball Association franchise. Oak Knoll (Hillsboro), Eyrie (Dundee), and Ponzi (Beaverton) wineries are founded. Powell's Bookstore opens. City riot police advance on war protesters at Portland State University, resulting in dozens of injuries.

1971

The Legislature passes, and Governor McCall signs, the bottle bill, the nation's first law requiring deposits on pop and beer containers. The World Forestry Center opens in Portland. The Legislature creates the Department of Human Resources and Children's Services Division. Blue Ribbon Sports becomes Nike. A single-member district reapportionment is established for the Legislature.

1972

Portland Center for the Visual Arts is founded. The State Forest Practices Act places strict controls on 11.7 million acres of nonfederal forestland.

1973

Lawmakers pass a landmark law creating statewide land-use planning. The Fremont Bridge is completed. Construction crews finish Portland's tallest building, the First National Center, now the Wells Fargo Tower. Pioneer Courthouse is restored. The Japanese-American Citizens League organizes. A new law reduces possession of less than an ounce of marijuana from criminal activity to an infraction, similar to a traffic ticket.

1974

Edith Green, who first went to Congress in 1954 by beating Tom McCall, decides to retire. Congress creates John Day Fossil Beds National Memorial. The Legislature authorizes the Oregon Government Ethics Commission. *Willamette Week* newspaper begins publication. Intel Corporation opens its Hillsboro plant. Boeing opens a Gresham plant.

1975

Portland State's Freeman Williams is NCAA Division I top basketball scorer; he'll repeat in 1978. Trojan Nuclear Plant begins operation. *One Flew Over the Cuckoo's Nest* is filmed at Oregon State Hospital.

1976

Yamhill District is added to the National Register of Historic Places. Portland City Council bans skateboards downtown.

1977

The Trail Blazers win the NBA world championship against Philadelphia. Siletz Tribes win back recognition and lands. The Legislature approves a ban on aerosol spray cans; creates Adult and Family Services Division, Workers' Compensation Department, and Metropolitan Service District. The Mittleman Jewish Community Center is dedicated. Mayor Neil Goldschmidt proclaims Gay Pride Day.

1978

Congress lists the Oregon Trail as a National Historic Trail. Voters approve the formation of the Metropolitan Service District (Metro). State statute restores the death penalty. Wacker Siltronic Corporation begins operations. A United Airlines DC-8 with 189 aboard crashes in East Portland, killing 10.

1979

President Jimmy Carter appoints Goldschmidt secretary of transportation. Blitz-Weinhard Brewery is sold to Pabst Brewing. An ice storm cripples the region.

Sy Vann (center), a Cambodian refugee, arrives in June 1979 in Portland, which became the home for thousands of Southeast Asian refugees. Vann, greeted by children and relatives, learned upon her arrival that her husband, whom she thought was dead, was alive in Thailand.

could not keep up. As demand for lumber increased, auction bids for federal timber soared during the 1970s. Few people worried. After all, the price of federal trees could climb because the growing demand for lumber and new housing seemed unlikely to stop.

And then it did.

END OF THE BOOM YEARS

The end of the 1970s for Oregon came on October 6, 1979, when an obscure committee in Washington, D.C., decided to raise the price of borrowing money. Today, news of the Federal Reserve Board's actions draws intense attention and speculation. Americans have learned the Fed's decisions on interest rates can whipsaw stock markets and the nation's feelings of prosperity. Not so in 1979. The anonymous Fed board worried about the way in which inflation in the 1970s had chewed away buying power. The then-Fed chairman, Paul Volcker, decided the nation needed a strong tonic for inflation: higher interest rates. Higher rates meant less borrowing from banks, and that meant less spending and less inflation.

VERA KATZ
Katz got her start fighting City Hall and now presides over it. After pushing neighborhood issues, Katz was elected to the Legislature in 1972. She rose to co-chair the budget-writing Ways & Means Committee by 1977, before becoming the state's first woman speaker of the House in 1985. Katz would push through the state's pioneering school reform before being elected Portland's mayor in 1992.

As interest rates rose, the roaring home-building industry didn't just cool, it froze. Demand for Oregon's lumber fell. Timber companies were stuck with high-priced logging contracts in federal forests just as demand for lumber vanished. The closing vise created by a dwindling timber supply and high interest rates shattered the Oregon economy. Within years, nearly half of the state's 80,000 timber jobs vanished and never returned.

The free and easy times of the 1970s—having borne progressive ideals and heroic moves to protect livability—deflated overnight. Oregon boarded up its pride like the shuttered windows of Main Streets in its rural timber towns. As the 1980s arrived, the courageous charge at building a better, smarter state turned to retreat as Oregon's leaders worried about keeping the state out of bankruptcy. Oregon once had laughed at keeping people out. Now it could not keep them in, as families fled small towns in search of survival.

One tale of those darkening days might be apocryphal, but there are those who swear they saw the signs nailed to lampposts of the small mill towns crushed by a new depression. The signs read: "Will the last one out please turn off the lights?"

Mount St. Helens blew 1.2 cubic kilometers of ash into the air and knocked forests flat for a dozen miles in an explosive eruption on Sunday morning, May 18, 1980. The volcano killed 57 people, most of whom thought they were beyond its reach.

BIG DEALS IN THE 1980s

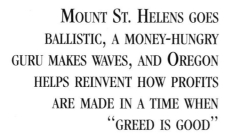

MOUNT ST. HELENS GOES
BALLISTIC, A MONEY-HUNGRY
GURU MAKES WAVES, AND OREGON
HELPS REINVENT HOW PROFITS
ARE MADE IN A TIME WHEN
"GREED IS GOOD"

By James Long

To the extent that a decade can be about anything, the 1980s were about money—money with lots of zeros. So many zeros that the only thing the money was good for, beyond a certain point, was to count it. Collecting money became a craze, and the more people collected, the more they wanted, and when they got that, they were crazy for still more. And so on.

Oregon helped launch a world belief that money could be created from nothing: "Big Bang" money. It did this by becoming the first state to use public pension money to finance corporate takeovers whose triple-digit killings sent Wall Street into a frenzy. This not only helped launch a national mania for free money but also reshaped the national culture in the form of a dollar sign.

Corporate raiders became celebrities, pushing Hollywood stars off magazine covers. Michael Douglas had to stalk around in yellow suspenders and say "Greed is good" to win an Oscar for a 1987 movie called *Wall Street*.

In Oregon, the money rush took many forms: timber cash-outs that erased communities, voter approval of legalized gambling to earn money for state expenses, the arrival of a Rolls-Royce-driving guru who converted bliss into money, and a symbolic rearrangement of Portland's skyline by a volcano that had figured in the nation's biggest land swindle.

PROFITS BEFORE PEOPLE

Oregon's role in the invention of the 1980s was to hand $202 million in the summer of 1981 to a small and virtually unknown New York investment firm, Kohlberg Kravis Roberts & Company. KKR specialized in "leveraged buyouts," a maneuver Wall Street old-timers called "bootstrapping." It was like buying a business and having the seller make the payments.

The bootstrapper would borrow (leverage) the purchase price with high-interest junk bonds, then retire the debt by selling parts of the company and squeezing higher profits from the rest. This usually meant cutting wages and benefits, firing people, and dipping into the company's pension fund.

The Oregon Investment Council, which oversaw investments for the state's Public Employees Retirement System, put up money in August and September 1981 for KKR to buy out Norris Industries, a Southern California toilet manufacturer, and Fred Meyer, the Portland-based retail chain. The returns were jaw-dropping, and Oregon through the 1980s would invest more than $1 billion in KKR buyouts.

Oregon's role was not an accident. While most other state pension funds were restricted legally to financial backwaters, Oregon rules permitted whitewater rafting. This suited Roger Meier, a canny Portland financier who served as the Oregon fund's chairman and who, when asked to describe his leadership style, told a reporter "benevolent dictator." It helped KKR's credibility that Jerry Kohlberg, a founder, had clerked for Portland's chief federal judge, Gus Solomon. And when KKR partner George Roberts explained how a leveraged buyout would work, Meier had no trouble seeing the potential.

Far left: *Downtown Portland remained a focus of revival in the 1980s, including opening the Portland Center for the Performing Arts in 1987.* Top: *Portlandia, Portland's best-loved statue, heads toward a rocky marriage in October 1985 with the city's least-loved building, the postmodern Portland Building.* Left: *In 1983, construction began on Pioneer Courthouse Square. About 63,000 citizens helped finance what became known as Portland's living room by buying bricks with their names stamped on them, at $15 apiece.* Above: *Overseeing much of the change was unorthodox Mayor Bud Clark, who, on any given day, might be seen canoeing on the Willamette.*

The Mount St. Helens explosion on May 18, 1980 battered forests as far away as 18 miles, flattening 230 square miles of trees around the blast.

KKR buyouts ranging from Safeway to RJR Nabisco yielded returns as high as 128 percent. But the financial results were almost incidental to the larger effects of KKR's success, which set off trends that changed the way businesses were managed. And this, in turn, changed American culture. The new way of managing companies focused on earnings and placed less emphasis on the social contract that bound workers and companies together, or companies and communities. "Lean and mean" became a credo; people were expendable. So the country turned a corner in the 1980s, and Oregon helped the country turn it.

The irony, said Ernie Englander, a professor of business at George Washington University who has studied KKR, is that public employee pension money was used to undermine the welfare of nonpublic workers whose taxes had financed the system.

"I don't think KKR was any better or any worse than anyone else," Englander said. "The bottom line is that the workers lost out."

PHIL KNIGHT
He steered Nike from a small start-up company to a world-wide icon. Known globally for its logo, "the swoosh," and criticized nationally for its overseas labor practices, Nike has made Knight one of the nation's richest men. He founded what would become Nike with his UO track coach, Bill Bowerman.

A MOUNTAIN OF A DEAL

Mount St. Helens was a perfect symbol for the change that the 1980s brought. Portlanders had pointed to the ice-cream peak with pride of ownership although it (a) stood in Washington, and (b) belonged to a private company, the Burlington Northern Railroad. How a railroad got title to the top of a volcano was the story of a land deal that the 1980s could appreciate.

Congress had deeded the summit to a Burlington predecessor, the Northern Pacific Railroad Company, as part of a 19th-century scheme to get a track built to the Pacific Ocean. The grant, containing enough land to form a state as big as Nebraska, was laid out like a 2,000-mile-long checkerboard along the right of way, with the railroad getting every other square to sell to settlers to pay for construction. But the Northern Pacific was not so much a railroad as a club of cronies who proved more adept at claiming federal real estate

Ron Herndon (standing, right) disrupts a March 29, 1982, Portland School Board meeting to protest the Tubman Middle School site, as new Superintendent Mathew Prophet (bottom right) watches. The board later agrees to place the school near Memorial Coliseum.

than laying track. When the rail line finally was completed, the taxpayers had been hornswoggled by the land grab. The checkerboard pattern of land ownership cut ecosystems into arbitrary parcels that gave rise to environmental problems that persist today. Burlington Northern came to own the mile-square piece atop Mount St. Helens, which was the one that fled in several directions in May 1980.

The blast was heard as far away as Redding, California. An ash cloud rose 80,000 feet in 15 minutes, and ash came down as far away as Kansas. Another 2.5 cubic kilometers ran away from the mountain in the form of a landslide. It was the biggest in recorded history, tumbling 17 miles along the north fork of the Toutle River.

Fifty-seven people died, including at least seven loggers on timberlands carved partly from railroad grants. The Washington Department of Natural Resources, which earned $175 million a year cutting timber, and the Weyerhaeuser Company, which owned a 473,000-acre tree farm around the west

J. E. "BUD" CLARK
A popular Portland saloon owner, Clark won his first of two terms as mayor in 1984. He made the controversial choice of Penny Harrington as the first woman to lead a major U.S. police force. On any given day, Clark might be seen entering City Hall in short pants, or pedaling fearlessly around a gang-infested neighborhood on his bike, or poling his canoe on the Willamette.

side of the mountain, had to choose between risking profits and risking loggers. They risked the loggers.

After an initial small eruption of ash on March 27, 1980, a bulge had grown on the volcano's north summit at the rate of several feet a day, and at 8:32 A.M. on the sparkling Sunday morning of May 18, an earthquake shook it loose. The bulge collapsed down the steep slope, exposing water-saturated magma that had been held in check by the sheer weight of the mountain. Without the weight pressing on it, the superheated water flashed to steam, atomizing the rock and causing part of the mountain to explode like an immense boiler. Steam and ash shot north at near-supersonic speed, a stone wind, hot enough to melt lead, that expanded like a nuclear fireball.

The stone wind is what killed most of the people who died. It lifted D-8 Caterpillars off the ground 10 miles from the crater, shredding solid steel to confetti. People had little chance.

Dave Johnston, a young government geologist, watched the mountain come toward him at a trailer

Bhagwan Shree Rajneesh with his chief aide, Ma Anand Sheela.

on a ridge five miles from the eruption. Johnston radioed, "Vancouver, Vancouver. This is it."

They never found his body.

The blast knocked down forest for 18 miles, clearing a fan-shaped area of trees over 230 square miles. Bill and Jean Parker had parked their pickup on Logging Road 3500 on a bluff facing the mountain that morning. When their bodies were found, Bill, a telephone worker, still had one hand on the steering wheel; Jean, a nurse, continued to sit with her arms folded. They were 10 miles from the volcano. Southwest of the bluff, near Fawn Lake, Christy Killian, 20, died clutching her white poodle. Her body was identified from her left hand, which bore her wedding ring and still lay on the dead dog.

On December 2, 1982, L. James Brady, vice president of timber and land for Burlington Northern, deeded Mount St. Helens' summit back to the United States, minus the 1,314 feet that had blown away, for inclusion in the Mount St. Helens National Volcanic Monument.

RAJNEESH ARRIVES

The mountain was still sputtering, and KKR was just beginning to tap Oregon pension money when a jet-setting guru named Bhagwan Shree Rajneesh hit the state. He brought hundreds of worshipful

NORMA PAULUS
Paulus would blaze trails for women throughout a 30-year public career. The moderate Republican joined the Legislature in 1970, latching on to both women's rights issues and the environmental movement. As the state's first woman secretary of state, she pushed vote-by-mail and protected the election process from abuse by Rajneeshees. After a grueling loss for governor in 1986, she passionately carried out pioneering school reform as the state's schools chief in the 1990s.

followers and a message that seemed right for the 1980s: "Jesus saves, Moses invests, Rajneesh spends." Money was good, Rajneesh announced, and so was sex—and the more of both the better.

Rajneesh—real name Mohan Chandra—attracted well-to-do followers; he said the rich deserved a guru, too. He collected Rolls-Royces, somewhere between 70 and 90 of them, and wore diamond-crusted Rolexes with his robes. Rajneesh started out by selling books of his writings out of the trunk of his Fiat around Bombay, India. Then he started leading wealthy women to enlightenment, and soon Western Europeans were showing up and demanding enlightenment, too. Rajneesh built up a commune before skipping to the United States in 1981, a step ahead of India's authorities.

Rajneesh and hundreds of followers installed themselves on a 100-square-mile ranch east of Madras, incorporating a city to get around Oregon's strict land-use laws. The mostly foreign-speaking Rajneeshees, clad in hues of red, worked around the clock to build Rajneeshpuram, complete with city hall, police department, shopping mall, hotel, airport, and casino.

U.S. immigration authorities began investigating citizenship fraud. In October 1983, Oregon Attorney General Dave Frohnmayer sued to dissolve Rajneeshpuram, saying the city blended church and state. Ma Anand Sheela, Rajneesh's chief aide, went

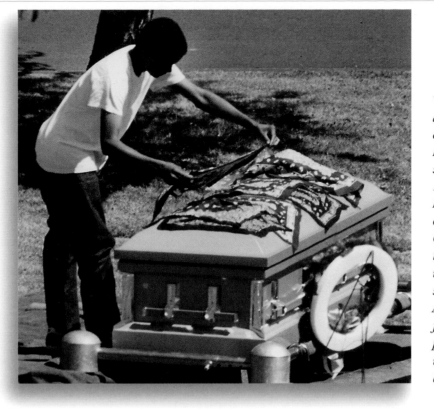

Violent street gangs and a crack cocaine epidemic caught Portland by surprise in the late 1980s. Joseph "Ray Ray" Winston, who called himself a Crips member, was the first of many victims of drive-by shootings. At his August 25, 1988, funeral, friends piled the casket with blue-trimmed bandanas.

on the air calling Oregonians "hicks" and "bigots." In January 1984, Sheela began installing phone taps and hidden microphones on the ranch, spending as much as $100,000 a month. She feared not only government agents but also rivals for power. The Rajneeshee security force bought 47 assault rifles and began practicing on human silhouette targets. Sheela and other leaders of the movement hatched a plot to take over Wasco County. They planned to rig the county government election by making other people sick to keep them from the polls. The Rajneeshees then would stuff the ballot boxes.

On September 12, 1984, the mayor of Rajneeshpuram and others tested the plan by sprinkling lab-cultured salmonella organisms on salad bars in four restaurants in The Dalles. About 750 people got sick in the largest biological attack ever known to occur on U.S. soil. That same month, Rajneeshees rounded up more than 3,000 homeless people from around the country and bused them to the ranch, where they were registered to vote. To keep them under control, some were fed Haldol, a powerful tranquilizer, in mashed potatoes. Amid accusations of attempted voter fraud, the Rajneeshees in October began dumping hundreds of the homeless on the streets in Portland.

Later Sheela and members of her circle allegedly plotted to murder Frohnmayer and other public

MARY DECKER SLANEY Slaney was America's best middle-distance runner of the 1980s and widely considered its whiniest and most star-crossed. Although Slaney set seven U.S. records and won the 1,500- and 3,000-meter races at the 1983 Helsinki World Championships, she never got an Olympic medal. The favorite in the 3,000-meter run in 1984, she tripped over barefoot South African Zola Budd, went sprawling and blamed Budd.

officials, and two Rajneeshees broke into the Wasco County courthouse and set fire to the planning office.

In the fall of 1985, however, the cult imploded in a power struggle that ended with Sheela and several others in prison. Rajneesh made a plea bargain to immigration fraud and was fined $400,000 and kicked out of the country.

GAMBLING, GANGS, AND CRACK

The Rajneesh imbroglio had diverted attention from other serious business in Oregon. In November 1984, Oregon voters approved a state lottery that began, modestly enough, as a sort of cash-prize turkey raffle. But soon the raffle morphed into big-time gambling. As the Legislature discovered the joys of taxless spending, it encouraged lottery officials to expand into keno, video poker, and sports bets. By the 1990s, Oregonians could gamble more ways than Nevadans, who lacked horse and dog tracks.

While Oregon expanded its gambling horizon, Congress passed a law in 1988 that said states could not forbid Native American tribes to offer whatever games the states permitted. Today, Oregon has eight tribal casinos, and they are big business, as is the Oregon State Lottery, whose staff now totals 410 employees, four times as many as work for the state Public Utility Commission.

PEOPLE

Population reaches 2,633,105 in 1980; 94.6 percent white.

HOME

In 1980, 14.8 percent of births in Oregon are to unmarried mothers; the rate rises to 25.3 percent in 1989.

The divorce rate from goes from 6.7 percent in 1980 to 5.4 percent in 1989.

In 1980, a four-bedroom home in Laurelhurst lists for $82,500; a three-bedroom ranch in Aloha costs $54,500.

Vine-ripened tomatoes cost 59 cents a pound; Red Delicious apples, 19 cents a pound; avocados, three for $1.

WORK

In 1980, Oregonians earn an average of $9,968; this rises to $16,387 by 1989.

In 1980, Oregon's minimum wage is $2.65 an hour for adults and $2.30 for minors; it rises to $3.85 for all by 1989.

Timber jobs vanish

As timber mills shut down or scaled back in the early 1980s, Oregon's unemployment rate climbed, dropped by the end of the decade.

Unemployment rate

12%

9   8.3%

6

4.2%

3

'80   '90
        Aug.

Source: Oregon Blue Book

PLAY

Portland celebrates its first Cinco de Mayo festival in 1985.

Oregon author Jean Auel publishes *Clan of the Cave Bear* in 1980, selling more than 20 million.

Seafood Mama becomes Quarterflash and lights up charts; Bruce Springsteen weds in Lake Oswego.

Stand by Me is filmed in Eugene, Cottage Grove, and Brownsville in 1985; Gus Van Sant's *Drugstore Cowboy* is filmed in Portland in 1988.

HEALTH

Oregon's first AIDS death occurs in March 1983.

GETTING AROUND

Oregon licenses 2.6 million autos in 1983, a million more than in 1974.

Delta Air Lines inaugurates Portland-Tokyo nonstop air service in 1987 and Portland-Seoul in 1988.

In 1989, Tri-Met transports 42.24 million riders on buses and 6.36 million by MAX train.

ENVIRONMENT

In 1983, the Legislature requires garbage services to offer curbside recycling.

In 1986, the state requires new wood stoves to comply with emission standards.

SCHOOL

Enrollment in 1980-81 is 520,000: 490,000 in public schools and 30,000 in private schools.

Tuition, fees, and room and board cost $5,580 at Oregon State University for 1986–87.

Oregon's high school dropout rate is 6.9 percent in 1988–89.

WAR

Ben Linder, Portland engineer, is killed in Nicaragua in 1987; he is considered the first U.S. citizen to die in the Contra-Sandinista war.

NATIONAL RANKINGS

30th-largest state in population and 39th in population density.

26th in per-capita income.

POLITICS

Democrat Michael Dukakis wins Oregon but loses the nation in the 1988 presidential race.

CRIME AND JUSTICE

The 1980s record 1,340 murders, compared with 1,089 in the 1970s.

CHURCH AND VALUES

In 1986, the Oregon Court of Appeals upholds a ruling that the inclusion of religious ceremonies at David Douglas graduation violates the Oregon Constitution.

As the state took to gambling in 1985, another sort of enterprise emerged: crack cocaine. Officials initially shrugged off the concerns of inner-city parents, but by 1987 it was clear that crack was different. It wasn't just a drug, but a business of gangs whose main attraction was that they provided a sense of belonging, in a society that seemed to have lost it.

The Crips and the Bloods were no longer just a California problem; they were a Portland problem. The City of Roses had become just another city of the 1980s, with better scenery.

On July 12, 1989, Mayor Bud Clark grimly accepted Governor Neil Goldschmidt's offer of the Oregon National Guard to assist the city police with the gang problem.

Oregon old-growth forests that once seemed limitless proved to have limits, after all. With their own big trees mostly gone, timber companies used political clout in the 1980s to cut public timber faster than it could be regrown.

RUNNING OUT OF OLD GROWTH

One other myth that fell hard in the 1980s was Oregon's self-image as a paradise of trees. In the 1980s, it became more a paradise of stumps. Through decades of overcutting, sawmills had largely run out of big, old-growth trees on their own property and had to cut younger trees at a rapid pace to stay in business. A review of Oregon harvest volumes on private lands in the 1970s and 1980s shows more acres being cut but less wood produced. "What that indicates," says conservation forester Roy Keene of Eugene, "is they got out of the big timber and started cutting the smaller second-growth; they had to cut a lot more acres to even keep up."

1980

Mount St. Helens blows its top, devastating 230 square miles of forestland, triggering floods, and killing 57. The depressed economy forces a special session of Legislature to cut $130 million from the budget. Paul Wenner serves up the first Gardenburger. Denny Smith ends U.S. Representative Al Ullman's 24-year House career.

1981

Followers of guru Bhagwan Shree Rajneesh buy the 64,000-acre Big Muddy Ranch in Wasco County. The State Supreme Court rules the death penalty statute unconstitutional. University of Oregon Health Sciences Center becomes Oregon Health Sciences University. Two officers dump dead opossums at an African American-owned restaurant in Portland, leading to a citizen committee to review police.

1982

Rajneeshees incorporate the city of Rajneeshpuram and begin a commune for 3,000. The Cow Creek Band of Upper Umpqua Indians wins recognition. Betty Roberts becomes the first woman onthe Oregon Supreme Court. Voters reject a property tax limit. The Legislature whacks $214 million from the state budget, and raises personal income and cigarette taxes and college tuition. The Oregon Journal publishes its last edition. Kohlberg Kravis Roberts & Company buys Fred Meyer.

1983

The Oregon Shakespeare Festival wins a Tony award. The Portland Winter Hawks win the Junior Western Hockey League championship. The Justice Center is dedicated. Former Governor Tom McCall dies at age 69. A Japanese freighter grounds at Yaquina Bay and spills thousands of gallons of fuel oil. Columbia Pacific Bank & Trust fails.

1984

Oregon voters approve a state lottery, reinstate the death penalty, and again reject 1 percent property tax limit. President Reagan signs the Oregon Wilderness Bill.

1985

Penny Harrington is named the city's first woman chief of police. The Blood and Crips gangs move into Portland. The Oregon State Lottery sells first instant-win tickets.

Bhagwan Shree Rajneesh, chief of staff Ma Anand Sheela, and commune depart in disgrace. Voters reject a sales tax.

1986

MAX begins Portland-Gresham service. China Gateway is dedicated. Seven students and two faculty members from the Oregon Episcopal School perish on Mount Hood. President Reagan signs the Columbia River Gorge National Scenic Area Act. Voters approve a $65 million Convention Center bond and the three-member Public Utility Commission.

1987

Oregon Vietnam Veterans Living Memorial is dedicated. Fire chars more than one-third of the Kalmiopsis Wilderness. Child-killer Diane Downs escapes but is recaptured 10 days later. The Portland Center for the Performing Arts opens.

1988

Grand Ronde tribes win nearly 10,000 acres. The Oregon Supreme Court affirms the death penalty. Eldridge Broussard Jr.'s dream of Ecclesia Athletic Association near Sandy collapses with the beating death of his daughter. Smoke from a burning field leads to 23-vehicle pileup, killing seven, on Interstate 5 near Albany.

1989

State Corrections Director Michael Francke is stabbed to death outside his Salem office. Oregon's worst serial killer, Dayton Leroy Rogers, is convicted of eight murders, including the 1986 "Molalla forest murders," and is sentenced to die. Congress compromises on preserving old-growth forests. White Stag leaves for Los Angeles.

A closed coastal timber mill where a former mill worker is employed as a security guard.

Many old-growth logs from private lands had gone overseas, not into U.S. housing. The reason was money. At the beginning of the 1980s, a 400-year-old, fine-grained Douglas fir log might bring $10,000 in Japan, but only $3,000 at a local mill. Domestic log prices were depressed because double-digit mortgage rates had driven home construction into the deepest decline since the Depression.

When the housing industry revived in the mid-1980s, mills that had overcut their own lands were lobbying to cut in the national forests. With jobs at stake, as well as profits, Senator Mark Hatfield, R-Oregon, and Representative Les AuCoin, D-Oregon, used their powerful committee positions to force the U.S. Forest Service to sell record numbers of trees. The Forest Service, critics charged, knowingly exceeded sustained-yield harvests for the first time.

"The forests really were raped in the 1980s like they never were before," said Bill Lang, a Portland State University history professor. "I would argue that the spotted owl crisis wouldn't have happened without this."

One of the casualties of the 1980s was the

JAMES DePREIST
Since arriving in 1980, DePreist has guided the Oregon Symphony through periods of confusion and financial disarray to a time of artistic stability and international recognition. He galvanized the orchestra and the community in the early 1980s by moving the part-time symphony into a full-time home, the Arlene Schnitzer Concert Hall.

company town of Valsetz, a sleepy possession of Boise Cascade in the Coast Range west of Salem. Valsetz had its own school team, the Cougars, and a library, and everybody knew everybody else. In February 1984, 96 people worked in the company veneer mill in Valsetz and lived, with their families, in company houses that rented for about $175 a month. The mill sat in the middle of company lands that once yielded big trees for saw-timber. Then the mill made plywood. Then it made just veneer sheets that it sent someplace else to make plywood. Then, that February, Boise Cascade called a meeting and said it was sorry, but the mill was losing money, according to the accountants, and everybody would have to leave. Veneers could be made more cheaply in Georgia, a company official explained.

As each family left, in the next few weeks, a company bulldozer would knock down the vacated house and push the rubble into a pile with the remains of other houses. On March 26, the company burned the rubble.

And it was about money. That's what the 1980s were about.

Workers clad in "bunny suits" walk through what has become Intel Corporation's new clean
room inside the new microchip development plant. By the mid-1990s, technology surpassed
timber as the state's top industrial employer.

THE BOOMING 1990s

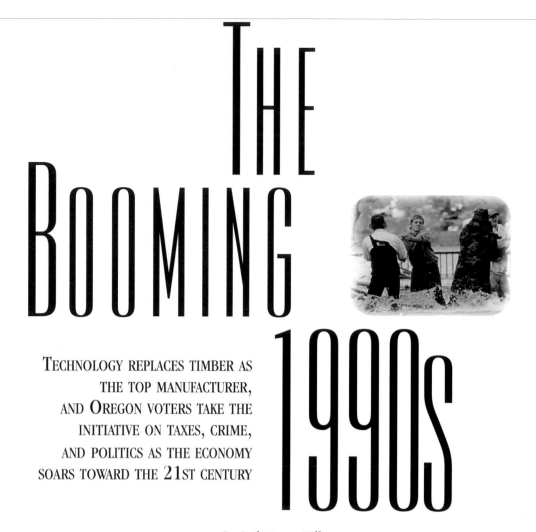

TECHNOLOGY REPLACES TIMBER AS THE TOP MANUFACTURER, AND OREGON VOTERS TAKE THE INITIATIVE ON TAXES, CRIME, AND POLITICS AS THE ECONOMY SOARS TOWARD THE 21ST CENTURY

By Gail Kinsey Hill

As the 1990s began, the northern spotted owl ruled Oregon. Declared threatened by the federal government, the shy forest creature became an unforgiving symbol of a state at odds with itself: a rich environment set against a troubled timber industry; an industrial heritage twisted toward an uncertain future; a proud, protective state divided by an angry citizenry.

Yet, as the forces fumed, a lesser-known denizen browsed the perimeter: a techno-bunny, ready to suit up for a takeover. The high-tech worker in clean-room garb would multiply, yes, like rabbits, depose the owl, shove aside timber, and become the symbol of an economic transformation.

Electronics manufacturers powered Oregon's economy in the 1990s to the forefront of a national expansion of record-breaking length. Led by Intel Corporation, high-tech flicked the spark for Oregon's boom times and provided the counterforce to the timber industry's downward spiral.

"Everything we were doing was starting to explode" in the early 1990s, said Keith Thomson, the reserved, lanky executive who oversaw Intel's Oregon operations and a mid-decade investment spree that would establish the Santa Clara, California–based chip-maker as a significant economic force.

Even so, the transformation was hardly transcendent. First, Oregonians struggled to shed the demons of the early-1980s recession. Then they struggled to adapt to all the growth, money, and change. Conflicts raged over how to pay for schools, how to protect the environment, how to deal with crowded roads and tightly packed neighborhoods— how, in short, to best get along.

What's more, the good times didn't roll for everyone. Much of rural Oregon played wallflower to the boom-time bash. The rich got richer at startling rates, while the average Joe barely beat out inflation. And a series of mergers and consolidations brought blandness to Oregon's landscape, just as a global economy promised greater diversity. As the decade closed, many Oregonians questioned whether the growth had buried their identity.

"Where's Oregon when it's all over?" asked Dan Wieden, a fourth-generation Portlander and the creative genius behind the Wieden & Kennedy ad firm.

ENDANGERED EMPLOYEES

Ernie Fegles lost his identity to the decade. Just out of Reedsport High School, he went to work at International Paper Company's paper mill a few miles north of home, along the wind-whipped Umpqua River in Gardiner. His grandfather had worked in the adjacent sawmill and his father in the plywood mill. New York–based International Paper owned all three mills and was the coastal community's largest and highest-paying employer.

By 1990, Fegles knew his job was in jeopardy. The spotted owl, recently protected under the Endangered Species Act, embodied some of the peril, but a host of other problems rattled the industry,

Above: *The westside light-rail tunnel became a technological feat and a pivot-point for controversy as Portland expanded MAX (Metropolitan Area Express) westward into Hillsboro. The five-year, $963 million project, with the deepest transit station in North America, was completed in September 1998.* Right: *A natural wonder—Keiko— drew thousands to his home at the Oregon Coast Aquarium in Newport.*

from years of overcutting and unreliable pulp supplies to nasty labor negotiations and foreign competition.

"No one wanted to believe the whole mill would shut down completely," Fegles said.

But in January 1999, after years of on-again, off-again operations, International Paper pulled the plug for good.

"It was a great job to have," said Fegles, who would find work as maintenance manager for Lower Umpqua Hospital in Reedsport. "The last of the great smokestack industries."

CHALLENGING THE SYSTEM

Fears that timber policies would throw the state into another recession swept through Oregon. No one wanted a replay of the early 1980s. They became defensive. They looked for ways to protect and control their lives. They looked for things to blame. Their mood, complicated by a rush of newcomers, erupted in politics, most notably in the state's initiative system and its promise of populist power.

Lon Mabon, the resolute director of the Oregon Citizens Alliance, went after gay and abortion rights; Don McIntire, a Gresham small-business owner, took aim at taxes; Frank Eisenzimmer, a firefighter-turned-activist, targeted politicians. Before the decade was half over, voters slapped in place tougher anti-crime laws, altered taxes, limited the terms of legislators, and gave the terminally ill the legal right to die with a physician-granted prescription. They did it with passion, even righteousness.

Perhaps no initiative represented the collective mood more than the property tax limits defined by 1990's Measure 5. By the beginning of the decade, Oregon had a full-blown tax revolt on its hands. Soaring home values had jerked up property taxes, and voters had grown tired of waiting for the Legislature to offer a fix. The Measure 5 campaign, led by a calmly defiant McIntire, tapped deep discontent by contrasting tax-weary homeowners with bloated government bureaucracies.

The establishment mounted a ferocious defense. If the measure passed, authorities warned, cash-stripped prisons would be forced to free criminals, fire departments would close fire stations, and police departments would slash patrols. In television ads, hordes of rats scurried into darkened streets as

New citizens are sworn in on May 3, 1990. Immigrants became part of the new face of Oregon in the 1990s, with 7,700 entering through the state in 1997 alone.

jail doors swung open. Chain saws ripped through police helmets, fire hoses, and schoolbooks.

"The onslaught was unbelievable," said McIntire, who liked to end a long day of campaigning with a single-malt scotch and a good cigar.

The measure passed with 52 percent of the vote.

No one felt more usurped than Barbara Roberts, a Democrat and Oregon's first woman governor. Roberts, a true believer in the helping hand of government, took office right alongside the initiative. Instead of beefing up programs, she found herself fighting to trim them down. Measure 5 wasn't Roberts's only problem. Timber interests, furious about her environmental positions, backed three recall attempts. She thought that her being a woman only sharpened their anger. Each time, the petition efforts fizzled, but rancor deepened.

"There was a huge anti-government sentiment," Roberts said.

Yet, she thought if she could only connect with the politically disenfranchised, she could change their minds and loosen their purse strings. She traveled the state asking voters what kind of a tax they wanted. She called her tour a "Conversation With Oregon." But few listened.

GUS VAN SANT
Van Sant began his film-directing career by taking bits of gritty Portland life and putting them into bizarre sketches of endeavor and irony. His breakthrough film was 1989's *Drugstore Cowboy*. He followed that success with *My Own Private Idaho, To Die For, Good Will Hunting,* and *Psycho*. At the center of the independent film scene, Van Sant refused to go truly Hollywood and clung to his Portland roots.

In fact, her solution, a sales tax, never reached the ballot. Larry Campbell, a Republican and the indomitable speaker of the House, killed the plan in a 1992 special session, dealing Roberts a serious political blow. Then, in 1993, the Legislature, badgered by special interests, offered its own version of a sales tax to the public. Voters trounced the proposal, marking the ninth sales tax defeat in the state's history.

Like a cat, the sales tax was good and dead, Oregonians joked.

CALIFORNIANS TO THE RESCUE

As it turned out, the state didn't need a big new tax to offset falling property taxes. Just as Measure 5's phased-in tax limits threatened to crimp the revenue flow, growth opened up full throttle. New home building and rising property values arrested a big slide in property tax collections. At first, population increases drove the runaway demand.

Californians, hit by a recession at home, turned toward Oregon in record numbers. Retirees poured into temperate coastal areas and Central Oregon's

Wearing a brilliant-blue costume and a determined look, Portland's Tonya Harding hit her triple jumps and a career high as she won the women's national figure skating title in Detroit in January 1994. Just days before, a man clubbed the knee of skating rival Nancy Kerrigan, and Harding, the ice world's bad girl, whirled into the Olympic Games amid the ensuing controversy.

When Kipland P. Kinkel opened fire in Springfield's Thurston High School on May 21, 1998, he shook a state and a nation. Kinkel killed his parents and two students and wounded 25, while shattering any sense among Oregonians that school shootings couldn't happen here.

high desert. Business people tapped the Willamette Valley's relatively cheap land and labor. Families looked to a gentler lifestyle.

Although the rest of the nation briefly dipped into a recession in 1991, chilled to contraction by the Persian Gulf War, Oregon barely sneezed. Income from taxes soared, fed by both the rising population and increased wealth. Collections rose by almost 70 percent between 1991 and 1998. Most significant to the state's tax structure, personal income tax collections surpassed property tax collections in 1994.

Now the income tax, arguably fairer but clearly more fickle, ruled. So when John Kitzhaber became governor in 1995, he faced a far different political and economic climate from his predecessor, Roberts, who, grieving the death of her husband, had decided against a re-election bid.

Kitzhaber enjoyed broad public support. A former emergency room doctor and state legislator, he liked to wear jeans and cowboy boots to work. On special occasions, such as his inaugural, he added a Jerry Garcia tie. He had a knack for bringing disparate interests together and forging

ARLENE SCHNITZER
When she founded a gallery near the waterfront in 1961, Schnitzer spawned a Portland art scene that grew to 200 galleries strong. A personal savior for hundreds of artists, she and husband Harold gave to more than 100 charities and public causes, from the Boys & Girls Clubs of Portland to the University of Oregon Judaic Studies Program to the performing arts center that carries her name.

a solution. But prosperity and a Republican-controlled Legislature frustrated his strengths. There was no sense of urgency from which to gain traction.

Kitzhaber vetoed bill after bill pushed through by Republicans, thwarting many a GOP objective and earning him the nickname "Dr. No." But Kitzhaber offered no bold initiatives of his own, a pragmatic nod to the state's growing complacency.

"This is a decade where we're delaying the day of reckoning," Kitzhaber warned.

In short, in the 1990s, the financial downside never came.

TECH INDUSTRY TAKES OVER

In 1995, the year after the income tax became revenue king, another transition occurred, one that changed the state's economic core.

Enter the techno-bunnies in droves. Employment in technology manufacturing computers, semiconductors, and test instruments—jumped 20 percent between 1990 and 1995. At the same time, timber reduced its workforce by 20 percent. When the

Volunteers and National Guardsmen fight to slow the Willamette and Tualatin Rivers, which poured into Lake Oswego and other cities in early February 1996. Warm weather and rains combined to push Northwest rivers over their banks. The Willamette reached its highest level in 32 years, coming within inches of breaching downtown Portland's reinforced harbor wall.

sawdust settled, technology had surpassed timber as the state's top industrial employer.

These were the years that semiconductor manufacturers plowed money into new computer chip fabrication plants. Intel, LSI Logic, Fujitsu Microelectronics, Wacker Siltronic, Mitsubishi Silicon America, among others, invested more than $10 billion in Oregon in 1995 alone.

Intel's contribution was Ronler Acres, a 250-acre site in Hillsboro. The state provided the carrot, with a tax break designed to lure continued investment by the likes of Intel.

Intel, which began investing in Oregon in 1974, quickly responded. In the three years after the 1993 tax law took effect, the company added 3,000 workers to its Oregon presence, an increase of more than one-third. It racked up $2 billion in capital spending. Ronler Acres would use Intel's most advanced manufacturing process and produce some of the company's fastest, most powerful microprocessors.

By the end of the decade, Ronler Acres, together with the other Oregon facilities, would represent Intel's largest investment in any single state, even

LUIS PALAU
Evangelist Palau took his crusade to millions of people all over the world and became recognized as the man most likely to succeed Billy Graham. A lively two-day event in Portland in the summer of 1999 drew 90,000 to Waterfront Park. Palau, born in Argentina, moved to the Portland area in 1978, basing his Evangelical Association in Cedar Mill.

greater than the company's California headquarters. The Oregon complex would employ 12,000 and become the state's largest industrial employer.

The electronics industry's capital spending billowed through the economy. In 1994, 1995, and 1996, Oregon's job count jumped by a startling 4 percent annually. In 1996 and 1997, Oregon's gross state product, the value of goods and services produced by a state, grew faster than that of any other state.

The boom pushed products far beyond Oregon borders. Businesses developed a voracious appetite for foreign markets, exporting goods to Canada, Asia, and Europe in record amounts. In 1997, the value of Oregon exports cracked the $10 billion mark, almost double 1990s' export total. Technology played into this record: Electronics manufacturers surpassed wood products and agriculture combined as the state's largest exporter.

"In 1989, if you said timber harvests would be cut in half," said Paul Warner, the state's chief economist from 1989 to 1999, "would you have ever thought we'd be the fastest-growing state in the country?"

PEOPLE

Population reaches 2,842,321 in 1990; Hispanic population increases 77 percent from 1990 to 1998, to 199,432.

Deschutes County grows by 31.4 percent between 1980 and 1996, the highest growth in the state.

HOME

The average home price in the Portland metro area is $96,329 in 1990 and rises to $181,000 in 1998.

0.9 percent of homes lack complete plumbing; 4.5 percent have no access to a telephone in 1990.

In 1990, 25.7 percent of Oregon births are to unmarried mothers; by 1997, it has risen to 28.8 percent.

Divorce rate falls from 5.5 percent in 1990 to 4.6 percent in 1997.

Most popular names for girls born in 1990: Jessica, Ashley, Emily, Sarah, Amanda; for boys: Jacob, Michael, Tyler, Joshua, Andrew.

WORK

In 1990, Oregonians earn an average of $17,423; by 1998 the average rises to $24,775.

In 1990, Oregon's minimum wage is $4.25 an hour; by 1999, it is $6.50.

In 1997, Oregon has 34,030 farms covering more than 17.4 million acres; in 1900, the state has 35,837 farms covering more than 10 million acres.

Timber harvests hit the lowest level in 70 years; in 1998 the total harvest is 3.53 billion board feet.

From timber to high tech
By the mid-1990s, jobs in high-tech manufacturing had overtaken the Oregon staple of lumber and wood products employment.

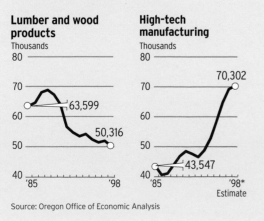

Source: Oregon Office of Economic Analysis

PLAY

8.3 million books were checked out of Multnomah County Library in 1997.

The Oregon Museum of Science and Industry's Gobi dinosaur exhibit attracts more than 575,000 visitors in 1997.

More than 50 movies were filmed in Oregon in the 1990s, including *Mr. Holland's Opus, Free Willy,* and *My Own Private Idaho.*

GETTING AROUND

In 1999, 4.1 million autos were licensed in Oregon; 218 licensed in 1905.

In 1999, Tri-Met carries 58.46 million riders on its buses and additional 17.9 million on MAX trains.

ENVIRONMENT

28 species, 19 animals and 9 plants, are listed as endangered or threatened, including northern spotted owl, coho salmon, marbled murrelet, Western snowy plover, and Western lily.

The Western pond turtle and Western painted turtle are down to less than 5 percent of populations that existed when the pioneers arrived.

SCHOOL

In 1990, 81.5 percent of Oregonians older than 25 have high school diplomas; 20.6 percent have a bachelor's degree or more.

In 1995, 576,557 students attend schools; 91.6 percent attend public schools; 6.6 percent attend private schools; and 1.8 percent receive home schooling.

WAR

Six Oregonians are killed in the Persian Gulf conflict in 1990–91.

NATIONAL FIRSTS

In 1998, 23 Oregonians fill prescriptions for lethal medications under the first physician-assisted suicide law.

In 1998, Oregon becomes the first state to conduct all elections by mail.

MEDICAL

By 1998, 4,363 AIDS cases are reported in Oregon; 2,615 result in death.

Attorney Morris Dees (right) *of the Southern Poverty Law Center relentlessly pursued Tom Metzger for civil liability in the 1988 death of Mulugeta Seraw. Metzger had recruited skinheads to his White Aryan Resistance and said after Seraw's slaying that "sounds like the Skinheads did a civic duty. On October 22, 1990, a Portland jury found Tom and his son John Metzger had incited the skinheads to murder.*

PUTTING DOWN ROOTS

If there was ever a poster-techie for the new and prosperous economy it could be Steve Grant, Ronler Acres plant manager. After the first phase of Ronler Acres opened in 1996, Grant stepped into the brick-and-glass building to run the show. Sandy-haired, clean-cut, and even-tempered, he wasn't yet 40. But he had worked for Intel for 16 years, hired fresh out of the University of Illinois in 1981, and he was star material.

Grant remembered clearly when he came to Oregon for the first time, in April 1981, for an interview with Intel. "It was so vividly green," he said. He took a trip to the coast. He drove to Mount Hood. He wanted the job.

Grant showed up for the interview at Intel's Aloha campus dressed in a dark blue suit, white shirt, and tie. Intel execs greeted him wearing jeans and polo shirts. They offered him an entry-level engineering job at $22,500 a year. No stock options.

Grant worked at Intel Oregon until higher-ups sent him to Albuquerque, New Mexico, in 1994 and then to Fort Worth, Texas, to oversee newly built facilities. But he kept his home in Oregon—"a very smart thing to do," he admitted, given soaring home

BARBARA ROBERTS Roberts, Oregon's first woman governor, tried to bring vision and direction to the mixed-up early 1990s. During her four years in office, she massaged Measure 5's property tax limits into the state's tax structure and pared expenses. She led the charge to revitalize the economy with the likes of Sony and Intel. Yet her liberal Democratic beliefs were ill-suited to an outraged timber industry and a conservative resurgence.

prices. Upon his return in 1997, he settled into his $350,000 home on 30 acres along Rock Creek Road west of Portland's urban growth boundary, the land-use line designed to help manage growth. He was only minutes from work, reaching his 9-foot-by-9-foot cubicle after a short commute along Cornelius Pass Road. Long ago, he gave up his business suits for khakis and polo shirts.

Now, Grant keeps his current salary and his stock options to himself, but he admits to plenty of both. Money isn't the point, he insists; it's happiness.

"I have a great family, a great job. I'm living where I want to live. This is my home. My roots are here."

NOT EVERYONE THRIVES

Yet as the decade closed, anxiety seeped more deeply into Oregonians' excitement about what the state was becoming. New people, new money, new technology, all rushing in without time for assimilation, compounded worries about the costs of so much change.

And not all were prospering. Although unemployment rates in the Willamette Valley remained

1990

U.S. lists northern spotted owl as threatened. Oregon Convention Center opens. Voters approve Ballot Measure 5, limiting property taxes. Pioneer Place opens. Detroit defeats Portland in National Basketball Association Finals.

1991

Barbara Roberts is inaugurated as Oregon's first woman governor. Frank Gable is convicted of murdering Corrections Director Michael Francke. The Legislature approves state-run video poker. AIDS is the No. 1 killer of men ages 25 to 44 in Multnomah County.

1992

Jim Hill is elected treasurer, becoming the first African-American in statewide office. Oregon Citizens Alliance's statewide anti-gay rights measure fails. A Multnomah County jury convicts Alberto Gonzales of spreading HIV, the first such case in the nation. Evangelist Billy Graham crusades in Civic Stadium. Chicago beats the Trail Blazers in the NBA Finals.

1993

Oregon becomes the first state with statewide vote-by-mail. Magnitude 5.6 earthquake causes $30 million damage in the northern Willamette Valley. The Oregon Trail turns 150. The Legislature bars local anti-gay-rights laws. Voters defeat a sales tax for the ninth time. Portland General Electric decommissions Trojan Nuclear Plant.

1994

Voters approve physician-assisted suicide. State's unemployment drops to 25-year low. Oregonians again reject OCA-driven anti-gay-rights measure. Dwindling salmon runs prompt ocean-fishing restrictions and a protection plan for the Columbia River basin. The State launches the Oregon Health Plan. The ambitions of Tonya Harding inspire an attack on Olympic skater Nancy Kerrigan. Nine Oregon firefighters die in a Colorado blaze. Penn State defeats Oregon, 38-20, in the Rose Bowl.

1995

U.S. Senator Bob Packwood resigns amid allegations that he sexually harassed more than two dozen women. Dammasch State Hospital closes after 34 years. The Rose Garden opens. Spirit Mountain Casino of the Confederated Tribes of the Grand Ronde opens.

1996

Douglas Franklin Wright is executed by lethal injection; it is the state's first execution in 34 years. Western Oregon is hit hard by floods. U.S. Senator Mark O. Hatfield retires after four decades as a public leader. Keiko, the *Free Willy* movie star, arrives in Newport. A federal provision allowing old-growth logging lapses after protests. Wells Fargo buys the First Interstate Bank.

1997

A ballot measure trying to repeal assisted suicide is trounced. First Bank System Inc. of Minneapolis buys U.S. Bancorp. The Nez Perce Tribe buys 10,000 acres and returns to Wallowa County.

1998

Kipland P. Kinkel kills his parents and then shoots up Springfield's Thurston High School, killing two students and wounding 25. Keiko flies to a new home in Iceland. Voters approve abandoning traditional polling, legalizing marijuana for medical purposes, and releasing birth information for adoptees. Tri-Met opens the Portland-Hillsboro MAX line.

1999

A federal jury penalizes anti-abortion activists $109 million for threatening abortion providers and posting the "Nuremberg Files" Web site. Nine West Coast salmon and steelhead runs are listed under the Endangered Species Act. The *New Carissa* runs aground near Coos Bay, leaking 70,000 gallons of oil. It beaches again after a failed tow attempt; a torpedo finally sinks it at sea.

On February 1993, U.S. Senator Bob Packwood disputes allegations of sexual misconduct and expresses confidence in receiving a "full and fair hearing" by the Senate ethics committee. On September 8, 1995, with that ethics panel recommending his expulsion, Packwood, 62, resigned, after 27 years in the Senate.

low, rates in many other communities hit double digits. Wages, adjusted for inflation, climbed in metropolitan Portland but fell elsewhere in the state. The currency meltdowns that strapped Asia singed export-reliant Oregon more than most of the nation. Shake-ups hit established Oregon companies as well as rooted individuals. As in perhaps no other decade, mergers and consolidations swept through the 1990s. In most cases, outsiders did the buying.

Houston's Enron Corporation bought Portland General Corporation in 1996, then three years later sold the local utility to Reno's Sierra Pacific Resources. Pennsylvania-based Rite Aid bought Thrifty PayLess. Phoenix-based DoubleTree bought Red Lion Inns. First Bank System Inc. of Minneapolis bought U.S. Bancorp. Cincinnati-based Kroger bought Fred Meyer Inc. ScottishPower PLC bought PacifiCorp.

"I don't think there's a strong sense of what it is to be an Oregonian anymore," said Chet Orloff, executive director of the Oregon Historical Society. "If you don't have that foundation to sink your roots into, you don't have that sense of place, that groundedness and commitment."

BILL SIZEMORE
As head of the Oregon Taxpayers United, Sizemore dominated the political initiative scene in the 1990s, fighting for lower property taxes, lower income taxes, less government regulation, and less union influence. A common-man embrace and an unflappable charm fueled his influence, but a past peppered with controversial business dealings and a dismal run for governor in 1998 picked at his popularity.

C. Scott Gibson, a co-founder of Sequent Computer Systems, flinched when he saw the IBM sign go up at the Sequent campus in 1999. "It's like one of your kids marries someone you don't know," he said.

Land and wildlife protections, established symbols of Oregon's covenant to guard its heritage, clashed with industrial and urban development like never before. Salmon, icon of Oregon's environmental integrity, struggled against extinction. The urban growth boundary, praised nationally as a visionary line-in-the sand against sprawl, began to fray, in concept and in practice.

Darrell Millner, a professor of black studies at Portland State University, watched as the land-use boundary and a rising demand for prime urban property transformed his Northeast Portland community into a new mix of shops, homes, and offices. He appreciated the activity but worried about the loss of deeply rooted neighborhoods. Millner doesn't look back with regret. But he hopes for a future with greater compassion for its past.

"If you go ahead without recognition of your heritage," he said, "then you will do a lot of damage and destruction."

INDEX

BIBLIOGRAPHY

The following is a selected bibliography of books on Oregon in the 20th century that reporters and researchers relied on heavily in preparing this project or were highly recommended:

Abbott, Carl. *Planning the Oregon Way: A 20-year Evaluation.* Corvallis: Oregon State University Press, 1994.

——. *Portland: Planning, Politics, and Growth in a Twentieth-Century City.* Lincoln: University of Nebraska Press, 1983.

——. *The Great Extravaganza: Portland and the Lewis and Clark Exposition.* Portland: Oregon Historical Society Press, 1996.

Applegate, Shannon. *Skookum: An Oregon Pioneer Family's History and Lore.* New York: Morrow, William & Company, Inc., 1990.

Beckham, Stephen Dow. *The Indians of Western Oregon: This Land Was Theirs.* Lake Oswego: Arago Books, 1977.

Buan, Carolyn M., comp. *The First Duty: A History of the U.S. District Court for Oregon.* Portland: Oregon Historical Society Press, 1993.

Corning, Howard McKinley, ed. *Dictionary of Oregon History.* Portland: Binford & Mort Publishing, 1989.

Dietrich, William. *Northwest Passage: The Great Columbia River.* Seattle: University of Washington Press, 1996.

Dodds, Gordon B. *Oregon: A Bicentennial History.* New York: W.W. Norton & Company, Inc., 1977.

——. *The American Northwest: A History of Oregon and Washington.* Wheeling: Forum Press, Inc., 1986.

Drukman, Mason. *Wayne Morse: A Political Biography.* Portland: Oregon Historical Society Press, 1997.

Gulick, Bill. *Roadside History of Oregon.* Missoula: Mountain Press Publishing Company, Inc., 1991.

Horowitz, David A., ed. *Inside the Klavern: The Secret History of a Ku Klux Klan of the 1920s.* Carbondale: Southern Illinois University Press, 1999.

Johansen, Dorothy O. and Charles M. Gates. *Empire of the Columbia: A History of the Pacific Northwest.* New York: Harper & Row, 1967.

Kesey, Ken. *Sometimes a Great Notion.* New York: Viking Penguin, 1977.

Long, James Andrew. *Oregon Firsts, Firsts for Oregon, Past and Present.* Cornelius: Pumpkin Ridge Productions, 1994.

Lowenstein, Steven. *The Jews of Oregon: 1850-1950.* Portland: Jewish Historical Society of Oregon, 1988.

MacColl, E. Kimbark and Harry H. Stein. *Merchants, Money, and Power: The Portland Establishment, 1843-1913.* Portland: Georgian Press Company, 1988.

——. *The Growth of a City: Power and Politics in Portland, Oregon, 1915-1950.* Portland: Georgian Press, 1979.

Marshall, Don B. *Oregon Shipwrecks.* Portland: Binford & Mort Publishing, 1984.

McKay, Floyd J. *An Editor for Oregon: Charles A. Sprague and the Politics of Change.* Corvallis: Oregon State University Press, 1998.

Moynihan, Ruth Barnes. *Rebel for Rights, Abigail Scott Duniway.* New Haven: Yale University Press, 1985.

Nash, Tom and Twilo Scofield. *The Well-Traveled Casket: A Collection of Oregon Folklife.* Salt Lake City: University of Utah Press, 1992.

Neal, Steve. *McNary of Oregon: A Political Biography.* Portland: Oregon Historical Society Press, 1985.

O'Donnell, Terence and Thomas Vaughan. *Portland: An Informal History & Guide.* Portland: Western Imprints, 1984.

O'Donnell, Terence. *Cannon Beach: A Place by the Sea.* Portland: Oregon Historical Society Press, 1996.

——. *That Balance So Rare: The Story of Oregon.* Portland: Oregon Historical Society Press, 1988.

Pitzer, Paul C. *Grand Coulee: Harnessing a Dream.* Pullman: Washington State University Press, 1994.

Robbins, William G. *Hard Times in Paradise: Coos Bay, Oregon, 1850–1986.* Seattle: University of Washington Press, 1988.

——. *Landscapes of Promise: The Oregon Story, 1800–1940.* Seattle: University of Washington Press, 1997.

Schoenberg, Wilfred P. *A History of the Catholic Church in the Pacific Northwest.* Washington D.C.: Pastoral Press, 1987.

Schwantes, Carlos A. *The Pacific Northwest: An Interpretive History.* Lincoln: University of Nebraska Press, 1989.

Snyder, Eugene E. *Portland Names and Neighborhoods: Their Historic Origins.* Portland: Binford & Mort Publishing, 1979.

Stafford, William. *Methow River Poems.* Lewiston: Confluence Press, Inc., 1995.

——. *The Long Sigh the Wind Makes.* Monmouth: Adrienne Lee Press, 1991.

Tamura, Linda. *The Hood River Issei: An Oral History of Japanese Settlers in Oregon's Hood River Valley.* Baltimore: University of Illinois Press, 1993.

Ulrich, Roberta. *Empty Nets: Indians, Dams and the Columbia River.* Corvallis: Oregon State University Press, 1999.

Walth, Brent. *Fire at Eden's Gate: Tom McCall & the Oregon Story.* Portland: Oregon Historical Society Press, 1994.

White, Richard. *The Organic Machine.* New York: Hill & Wang, Inc., 1995.